José Revueltas

Twayne's World Authors Series

Luis Dávila, Editor
Indiana University

TWAS 683

JOSÉ REVUELTAS
(1914–1976)

José Revueltas

By Sam L. Slick
Sam Houston State University

Twayne Publishers • Boston

José Revueltas

Sam L. Slick

Copyright © 1983 by G. K. Hall & Company
All Rights Reserved
Published by Twayne Publishers
A Division of G. K. Hall & Company
70 Lincoln Street
Boston, Massachusetts 02111

Book Design by Barbara Anderson

Printed on permanent/durable acid-free
paper and bound in the United States of
America.

Library of Congress Cataloging in Publication Data

Slick, Sam L., 1943–
  José Revueltas.

  (Twayne's world authors series. Mexico)
  Bibliography:
  Includes index.
  1. Revueltas, José, 1914–1976—Criticism and
interpretation. I. Dávila, Luis. II. Title.
III. Series.
PQ7297.R383Z88   1983   863   82-15474
ISBN 0-8057-6530-1

This book is dedicated
to my parents
Harvey and Emily Slick

Contents

About the Author

Born in Oelwein, Iowa, in 1943, Sam L. Slick received the B.A. and M.A. degrees from Illinois State University and the Ph.D. from the University of Iowa. In addition, he studied at the University of Madrid and Universidad Iberoamericana in Mexico City. He is currently an Associate Professor of Spanish and the Director of the International Archives of Latin American Political Posters at Sam Houston State University. Professor Slick's articles and reviews have appeared in Chasqui, Hispania, World Literature Today, Revista Chicano-Riqueña, and Review of the Center for Inter-American Relations.

Preface

José Revueltas participated in Mexico's intellectual and literary life for more than four decades. As one of his country's leading Marxist thinkers and activists he contributed greatly to the formation of contemporary leftist politics in Mexico. As a university lecturer he influenced the thought and literature of Mexico's young intellectuals and writers. But it was as an author that Revueltas most asserted his creative genius. In addition to his work as a journalist and a film scriptwriter for Mexican cinema, Revueltas left a rich and voluminous legacy of literature. He produced seven novels, four of which may justly be considered of capital importance either for historical or artistic reasons. He wrote over forty short stories, many of which are routinely cited today as masterpieces. One of his four plays held box-office records for over two decades in Mexico. Finally, as a prolific essayist, he wrote volumes on such topics as nuclear war, education, politics, society, film and revolution. In all, the thoughts expressed in his writings and in other endeavors helped transform the nature of twentieth-century Mexican literature.

In spite of his tremendous contributions, however, literary historians and critics, either purposely or inadvertently, paid scant attention to José Revueltas prior to his death in 1976. Subsequent to his death, however, the number of critical essays and books treating Revueltas's life and works has increased dramatically. Thus, after a period of astonishing neglect, Revueltas's role in Mexican literature has only recently been given proper attention. Not surprisingly, the prevailing critical consensus supports the view that Revueltas occupies a central position in Mexican letters. There has been, therefore, a radical recasting of Revueltas as a major figure in contemporary Mexican literature.

The present study is unique in at least two respects. First, it is the only existing study of Revueltas's literature that treats all four genres in which Revueltas seriously dedicated himself. It therefore includes the only published study ever made of his theater, and it contains the only comprehensive examination of his essays. Second, thanks to the active collaboration of Revueltas's wife, daughter, and son-in-law, this book contains what is currently the most extensive and authoritative biography of Revueltas. In addition, considerable detail has been given to an examination of how the author's personal life affected his literary production. Nevertheless, many biographical data were omitted for reasons of space. At the outset of this project, certain limitations were established. Revueltas's poetry, which was occasional and of minimal importance, was not included in the study. His film scripts, although numerous, were also excluded because they were deemed of marginal interest in relation to the works examined here. Every attempt for biographical and bibliographical accuracy was made. Factual information included in this study has been checked and rechecked rigorously for accuracy, and all errors must be attributed to the author.

This book, then, attempts to survey panoramically the novels, short stories, theater, and essays of José Revueltas. There has been no attempt to analyze his works from any particular point of view or according to the tenets of any specific school of literary criticism. Rather, the approach is decidedly historical, descriptive, and impressionistic. The organizing and guiding principle has been to provide a readable introduction to the topic. Pursuant to editorial guidelines, this study is directed to a non-specialized audience that, it is assumed, has little, if any, familiarity with Revueltas's literature. The initial chapter deals with Revueltas's life. Subsequent chapters are devoted to specific genres: novels, short stories, theater, and essays. While virtually all of the major works have been treated, some minor works have not been mentioned because of limitations.

I first became acquainted with José Revueltas through his literature in a graduate seminar, conducted by Professor Julio Durán-Cerda, at the University of Iowa in 1971. So struck was I by Revueltas's narrative that I elected a study of his novels as the topic for my doctoral dissertation some three years later. During this time, under the direction of Professor Oscar Fernández, my interest in Revueltas grew exponentially. In 1975, and again in 1976, I had the honor of meeting and visiting privately with José Revueltas in Mexico City.

This project has been possible only with the help, counsel, and support of a host of people. They are deserving of generous thanks. In particular, I extend warm appreciation to Professor Richard Cording, Dean of the College of Arts and Sciences of Sam Houston State University, for his encouragement and support. For careful preparation of the manuscript I thank Marta Vargas, Carol Popham, and Norma Gonzales. The securing of important documents, biographical information, and research materials was essential. For extraordinary help in this regard, I thank Carolina Cañas and Eloína Moreno Blanco of Mexico City and Ann Hartness-Kane, the Assistant Head Librarian of the Benson Latin American Collection of the University of Texas at Austin. I also wish to recognize the generous aid of Professor Marilyn Frankenthaler of Montclair State College for providing numerous research documents. Special mention must be made of the tremendous help afforded me by José Revueltas's daughter, Andrea Revueltas, and his son-in-law, Philippe Chéron, of Mexico City. For many hours of sharing personal information concerning José Revueltas, I am indebted to his wife, Ema Barrón, of Oakland, California. My appreciation is extended to those people who willingly and critically read the manuscript: Professor Timothy Murad of the University of Vermont, Barbara Gibson of Simpson College, Pamela Milutin of the University of Kentucky, Professor Elizabeth Fonseca-Downey, and Sheila Boydstun and Matt Golley of Sam Houston State University. My profound gratitude goes to Professor Robert Price, Coordinator of the Foreign Language Program at Sam Houston State University, whose many suggestions were eagerly incorporated into the text. A special thanks to Professor Luis Dávila for his careful reading of the manuscript.

Finally, I would like to thank my research assistant, Miss Marilyn Pletcher, now of the University of Michigan, who gave so tirelessly to this project in so many ways, and without whose help this book would not have been possible.

Sam L. Slick

Sam Houston State University

Chronology

1914   20 November: José Revueltas Sánchez is born in Durango, Mexico.

1920   The family moves to Mexico City and José enters the Colegio Alemán.

1924   José's father dies and the children are transferred to a public school.

1929   Arrested and sentenced to a federal reformatory for six months for his role in a political demonstration.

1930   Admitted to the Mexican Communist party in August.

1932   Arrested for participation in a labor strike, convicted, and sent to the Islas Marías for five months.

1934   Arrested in May for a strike in Anáhuac, Nuevo León, and sent to the Islas Marías for ten months.

1935   Released from the Islas Marías in February. Attends the Seventh World Communist Congress, from July to November, as a delegate for the Mexican Communist party.

1937   Marries Olivia Peralta in May.

1938   Publishes his first short stories.   Writes his first novel, El quebranto (The Surrender), but the work is stolen before being published.

1939   José's mother dies.

1940   Begins work as an apprentice journalist for El Popular.

1941   Los muros de agua (Walls of Water).

1943   El luto humano (The Stone Knife). Wins
        the Mexican Prize for Literature.
        Expelled from the Mexican Communist
        party.

1944   Dios en la tierra (God on Earth).   Writes
        his first film script, El mexicano.
        Helps establish an independent Marxist
        group, El Insurgente.

1945   Works with Mexican film director
        Roberto Gavaldón.

1946-   Works with Ignacio Retes and the theater
1950   group La Linterna Mágica.

1947   Divorces Olivia Peralta and marries María
        Teresa Retes. Participates in the
        Conferencia de Mesa Redonda, convened by
        Vicente Lombardo Toledano. Finishes the
        manuscript for Israel in May and
        Los muertos vivirán (The Dead Will Live)
        in August.

1948   Helps found the Popular party with
        Lombardo and Ramírez y Ramírez.
        Israel debuts in Mexico City.

1949   Los días terrenales (Earthly Days).

1950   El cuadrante de la soledad (Quadrant of
        Solitude) debuts in Mexico City in May.
        Revueltas publicly denounces Los días
        terrenales and El cuadrante
        de la soledad in June.

1953   Works with Luis Buñuel on La ilusión viaja
        en tranvía.

1955   Abandons the Popular party and formally
        seeks readmission to the Mexican
        Communist party.

1956   En algún valle de lágrimas (In Some Valley
        of Tears). Readmitted to the Mexican
        Communist party in March.

1957   Los motivos de Caín (The Motives of
        Cain). Travels to Europe and the Soviet

Union.

1958   *México: una democracia bárbara* (Mexico: A Barbarous Democracy)

1960   *Dormir en tierra* (To Sleep on Earth). Expelled from the Mexican Communist party in April and joins the Mexican Workers-Farmers party (Partido Obrero Campesino Mexicano). Abandons the POCM and creates the Liga Leninista Espartaco in September.

1961   Travels to Cuba as a film consultant for the Instituto Cubano de Arte e Industria Cinematográficos.

1962   *Ensayo sobre un proletariado sin cabeza* (Essay Concerning a Headless Proletariat).

1963   Expelled from the Liga Leninista Espartaco in June.

1964   *Los errores* (Errors).

1965   *El conocimiento cinematográfico y sus problemas* (Theory and Problems of Film).

1967   Awarded the Xavier Villaurrutia Literary Prize for his *Obra literaria* (Literary Works).

1968   Travels to Cuba in March, against the Mexican Government's wishes, as a literary judge for the Casa de las Américas. 2 October: the Tlatelolco massacre. 16 November: arrested for his participation in the Mexican Student Movement. 22 November: formally charged and sent to Lecumberri Prison to await trial.

1969   *El apando* (Isolation Cell).

1970   17-18 September: endures an uninterrupted, forty-hour trial. 12 November: formally sentenced to sixteen years in Lecumberri.

1971   Divorced from María Teresa Retes.

	13 May: released from Lecumberri Prison in ill health.
1972	Visiting lecturer at Stanford University from March to June.
1973	Marries Ema Barrón in August.
1974	<u>Material de los sueños</u> (Dream Matter). Holds position at the University of California at Berkeley as a visiting professor.
1975	Travels to Cuba at the request of President Echeverría. <u>Pito Pérez en la hoguera</u> (Pito Pérez in a Fix) debuts in August in Mexico City. <u>Antología personal</u> (A Personal Anthology).
1976	14 April: dies of a heart attack in Mexico City.

Chapter One

José Revueltas:
His Life and World

José Revueltas's life was often shrouded in mystery and controversy. Thoroughly a man of action, he was often forced to live on the margins of society for both social and political reasons. At the same time, however, he actively participated in Mexico's intellectual and public life. As one of his country's foremost theoreticians of radical politics, he provoked fear and hatred in many established spheres of Mexican society. On the other hand, for many Mexicans his life and ideas were a source of affection and hope. While his enemies sought continually to discredit him, his admirers tended to elevate him to the status of a folk hero. By any standard of measurement, however, José Revueltas's life was legendary.

Because Revueltas's existence was one of drama and intrigue, it is often difficult to separate fact from fiction concerning his many activities and exploits. Indeed, there remain entire segments of his life for which there is little concrete information available. Unfortunately, the author himself did little to clarify matters, for he openly disdained talking about his own life. Although he was often encouraged to write his memoirs, he died without doing so. On only one occasion did he offer the public an autobiographical sketch with his "Las evocaciones requeridas" (Required Evocations).[1]

That essay is of limited interest, though, since it deals only with his childhood. Thus, a biography must be gleaned from interviews, letters, newspaper reports, government documents, and the recollections of family and friends.[2] In this way, there emerges a profile of an extraordinary man whose life was marked by extraordinary personal and historical events.

Childhood and Adolescence, 1914–1930

José Revueltas was one of eleven children born to José Revueltas Gutiérrez and Romana Sánchez Arias of Santiago Papasquiaro, Durango. The father was a moderately successful grocery store owner who apparently preferred poetry to business. The mother, daughter of a Mexican miner, was a sensitive and intelligent woman who cultivated in her children a love for truth and the arts. She had hoped to produce an artist among her offspring. Interestingly enough, she bore four children who excelled in four different artistic media.
The Revueltas name is illustrious in twentieth-century Mexican history. No other family has given so much to the national arts. José's oldest brother, Silvestre, was one of Mexico's greatest musicians and composers. It was Silvestre who helped establish the family name as being synonymous with radical politics through his involvement in the Liga de Escritores y Artistas Revolucionarios. Another brother, Fermín, distinguished himself as a muralist; he was associated with such painters as Diego Rivera, David Alfaro Siqueiros, and José Clemente Orozco. Finally, Rosaura Revueltas is one of Mexico's most

notable film and stage actresses.

José was born on 20 November 1914 in Durango. His memories of his home town were clouded, however, for the family moved to Mexico City in 1920. In spite of financial restrictions, the parents assiduously insisted on the best education available for their children. Both Silvestre and Fermín, for example, had been sent to Saint Edward's University in Austin, Texas, as a means of avoiding the seriously disrupted Mexican schools during the Revolution. The young José, along with his sisters, entered the Colegio Alemán, one of Mexico City's finest private elementary and secondary schools. But José proved to be a rebellious and inattentive student. The restrictive environment of the Colegio Alemán was not conducive to his inquiring mind.

In 1924, with the death of the father, the family's fortunes abruptly changed. Facing a critical financial crisis, the mother transferred the Revueltas children to a public school. Although José fared somewhat better in his new school, he was already well on the road to self-instruction. He read voraciously and eclectically, drawing on texts from his father's library, as well as those of his brothers. As the family's hardships mounted, there was a loosening of the once close-knit bonds that had characterized the Revueltas family. At about the age of thirteen, José began to work parttime for a hardware distributor. He was placed in direct contact with older laborers, including a certain Manuel Rodríguez, nicknamed "Trotsky," who lectured the workers on Marxist theory. So captivated was Revueltas by the lessons in Marxism that he later recalled having prophetically observed that "This deserves the devotion of my entire life."[3] The making of a young Marxist radical was in process. These early lessons were to govern his artistic, political, and social life for some fifty years. It was from these informative lectures that Revueltas began to formulate his ideas on equality, justice, and society.

While still fourteen years of age, Revueltas attended a political demonstration at the Zócalo in downtown Mexico City. José was promptly arrested for his participation and, because he was a minor, was sent to a federal reformatory for ten months. This incarceration was to be the first of many throughout his life for political reasons. It was this first imprisonment, however, that was to be so crucial, for it placed Revueltas amid an element of Mexican society generally unknown to him. During his stay in the reformatory, his still freshly acquired Marxist philosophy took on new meaning.

The Communist Party and the Writer, 1930–1943

After his release from the reformatory, Revueltas never returned to formal education. He worked at various jobs while maintaining numerous contacts with leftist radicals and labor union organizers. He first joined the Socorro Rojo, an ancillary arm of the Partido Comunista Mexicano (Mexican Communist party), and then, in 1930, after a probationary period, was admitted directly to the PCM (Mexican Communist party). This move was a bit unusual in that Revueltas bypassed the Communist Youth party entirely. According to the author himself, it was apparent that his very literate background made him unacceptable for the less sophisticated activities of the Communist Youth party. Two years later, in 1932, Revueltas organized a strike at El Buen Tono, a Mexico City factory. Arrested for his part in the strike, he was sentenced to the infamous penal colony of the Islas Marías, where he spent some five months. His release was brought about by the prison director, the revolutionary leader General Francisco Mújica, who was an acquaintance of the Revueltas family.

Revueltas returned to Mexico City in ill health, having contracted malaria on the Islas Marías. As circumstances permitted, he began to do field work for the Party by operating as a labor organizer in rural states like Veracruz and Yucatán. In 1934 he was sent by the Party to Anáhuac, Nuevo León, to organize a major strike. He was once again arrested and sent to the Islas Marías.[4] After serving nearly ten months, he was released in February, 1935. Now an important member of the Mexican Communist party, he was sent to the Soviet Union as a delegate to the Seventh World Communist Congress. While abroad he learned of Fermín's death.

The years from 1938 to 1941 represented a period of great literary activity punctuated by personal tragedy. In 1937 he had married Olivia Peralta, the first of three wives he was to have.[5] This marriage produced four children.[6] Apparently the new stability afforded him as a married man, plus new responsibilities, provided a lifestyle in which he could develop his literary tendencies. Revueltas began to publish numerous short stories which appeared in a variety of journals including Ruta, Tierra Nueva, and Romance.[7] He formed many important literary friendships through his association with the writers of Taller.[8] In 1939

Revueltas wrote his first novel, El quebranto (The
Surrender), based on his experiences in the federal
reformatory. Unfortunately, the manuscript was
stolen before it could be published.[9] This event
did not discourage Revueltas, though, for he was
about to launch a lengthy and distinguished career
in literature. With the financial help of his family
he was able to publish his first novel, Los muros
de agua (Walls of Water), in 1941. This work was
based on his previous two visits to the Islas Marías.
Along with Revueltas's growing literary success
there was a series of personal tragedies. His
mother died in 1939. The following year he lost
his sister, Luz, and his brother Silvestre. The loss
of Silvestre, a veritable national hero, affected
José deeply.

During this same period Revueltas took a job as
a reporter for El Popular.[10] He was first hired as
a ruletero, a kind of roving reporter who covered a
multitude of events. He was subsequently given his
own column, "La marea de los días," which ran
from 1941 until 1942.[11] In 1945 he was given
other columns, although they were shortlived.
Quite aside from the journalistic value of these
columns, the assignments undoubtedly enriched
Revueltas's personal knowledge of widely disparate
segments of Mexican society, thus setting the stage
for many of his subsequent fictional narrations.

The year 1943 was one of both crisis and
triumph for José Revueltas. He saw the
publication of his now-famous El luto humano (The
Stone Knife).[12] Prior to its publication, the novel
was awarded the Premio Nacional de Literatura and
was selected as the Mexican entry in the Pan
American literary contest sponsored by Farrar and
Rinehart of New York. Yet, while the literary
world was lauding his new novel, Revueltas was

suffering a serious political setback. The author, along with other members of the José Carlos Mariátegui Cell, was expelled from the Mexican Communist party. In response to his expulsion, Revueltas began a personal campaign to create a new party that would effectively represent Marxist interests and the proletariat. This struggle, which would last for many years, involved a variety of activities.

The Literature of Revisionism, 1944–1950

Revueltas's political activity outside the Communist party represented, in large part, the prima materia of his private and public life for some three decades. Most of his involvement was directed toward one of two possible goals. Either he would persuade the Mexican Communist party to reform by adopting "true" Marxist principles or he would supersede the Party by creating a more authentic one. His first initiatives occurred between 1940 and 1943, while still in the Party. Shortly before his expulsion in 1943, Revueltas, along with two colleagues, Enrique Ramírez and Rodolfo Dorantes, began to publish a shortlived opposition journal titled El Partido.[13] In the following year he continued his revisionist activities, now outside the Party, by helping create an independent Marxist group, El Insurgente. The result was yet another opposition journal, El Insurgente. It was becoming clear to Revueltas, however, that his militant publications and activities lacked effectiveness, and that something more radical was required if the Mexican Communists were to listen to his message of reform.

In the meantime, Revueltas published his first collection of short stories, <u>Dios en la tierra</u> (God on Earth), in 1944. In the same year he began a career as a scriptwriter for the Mexican film industry, an occupation that he was to pursue until the 1960s.[14] In all, Revueltas produced scripts for nearly thirty films. His cinematographic career involved collaboration with such directors as Julio Bracho, Miguel Morayta, Roberto Gavaldón, and Luis Buñuel. Although Revueltas at times openly disdained his participation in the world of cinema, in retrospect, his film career takes on significant dimensions. Not only was he an important influence within the Banco Cinematográfico (National Cinematographic Bank), but he wrote on the theory of film and even taught scriptwriting at the National University of Mexico. Perhaps his most important legacy to Mexican film was his undaunted struggle against monopoly and censorship in the industry.

In 1945 Revueltas reestablished himself briefly with <u>El Popular</u> by writing two different columns: "Los episodios nacionales," and "Caminos de la nacionalidad." In 1946 he entered still another artistic arena by associating himself with the Mexican stage director Ignacio Retes and the theatrical group La Linterna Mágica. The eventual result was the creation of five plays, only three of which have ever been produced.[15] It was through Ignacio Retes that Revueltas met the director's sister, María Teresa Retes, whom he married in 1947, shortly after divorcing Olivia Peralta.

While Revueltas was working in both cinema and theater, he continued an active political life. In the process of his revisionist activities, he became convinced of the uselessness of the Mexican Communist party. In January 1947 he participated in the Conferencia de Mesa Redonda convened by the flamboyant labor leader Vicente Lombardo Toledano.[16] Along with Toledano and Ramírez y Ramírez, Revueltas helped establish the Popular party in June 1948. The new party, which was based upon the needs of the petite bourgeoisie, would not, ultimately, serve Revueltas's ideals and goals. But it seemed an effective means with which to counter the leadership of the Mexican Communist party.

In 1948, Israel, Revueltas's first play, debuted for a short run in Mexico City. In 1949, Los días terrenales (Earthly Days), his third novel, was published. This work was met with immediate criticism by leftist colleagues for its unrelenting attack upon the Mexican Communist party. The criticism against Revueltas peaked in 1950 with the debut of El cuadrante de la soledad (Quadrant of Solitude), the first Mexican play to achieve one hundred consecutive performances. While Earthly Days was criticized for its political content, Quadrant of Solitude was viewed as a Sartrean existentialist work and, consequently, as being diametrically opposed to Socialist Realism, the prevailing Marxist artistic schema.[17] It was at this juncture that one of the most curious developments in Mexican literature occurred. As published attacks against Revueltas mounted, especially those of Juan Almagre and Enrique Ramírez, Revueltas openly denounced his own works by publishing a letter in which he called for the voluntary withdrawal from sales of Earthly Days, and the cessation of performances of Quadrant of Solitude, because the two works reflected "misguided" judgments.[18]

Political Soul-Searching, 1951–1967

The period from 1951 to 1955 represented a time of relative dormancy for the writer. Although Revueltas wrote several short stories and a short novel, he concentrated primarily on movie scripts. It was clearly a time of confusion and great soul-searching. Ironically, however, it was a period of economic prosperity; Revueltas earned considerable money through his work in films, which permitted him a life-style not previously known to him. This momentary period of some affluence, however, was uncharacteristic of Revueltas, the selfless Marxist, who disavowed material wealth.

In 1955, after years of polemics and disagreements with Toledano, Revueltas announced his separation from the Popular party. At roughly the same time he formally sought readmission to the Mexican Communist party. He was reinstated the following year. In 1956 he published his fourth novel, En algún valle de lágrimas (In Some Valley of Tears), as well as a monograph titled El realismo en el arte (Realism in Art). In addition, he wrote a highly political play titled Nos esperan en Abril (They'll Be Waiting for Us in Abril).[19] During the following year, Revueltas made his second trip to the Soviet Union, this time to promote a film project. In the same year, he published his fifth novel, Los motivos de Caín (The Motives of Cain).

Revueltas had reentered the Mexican Communist party with the hope of restructuring the Party's methods and goals in order to create a truly representative party of the proletariat. He was on a collision course, however, with the political realities of Mexico. In 1960 he was once again

expelled from the Party for his revisionist
tendencies. He then joined the Mexican
Workers-Farmers party, but abandoned it after
several months. In a final desperate attempt to
form an authentic Marxist party, he then founded
the Liga Leninista Espartaco. But this group
quickly adopted a Maoist position, against
Revueltas's wishes, and expelled him in 1963. With
this last episode, the writer's long term
involvement in political parties came permanently
to an end. Nevertheless, he remained Mexico's
most important Marxist idealogue until his death.

Curiously, after being expelled from the
Communist party, Revueltas traveled to Cuba in
1961 as a film consultant for the Instituto Cubano
de Arte e Industria Cinematográficos. While there,
he fell in love with Omega Agüero, a Cuban
woman, by whom he had a child. From 1958 to
1964 Revueltas produced numerous works of both
fiction and nonfiction. In 1960 he published his
second collection of short stories, Dormir en tierra
(To Sleep on Land). During this period he worked
diligently on a new novel, Los errores. Revueltas's
most important literary works during this period,
however, were in nonfiction; he wrote and published
many important political essays, monographs, and
books. Of these, perhaps the two most impressive
were México: una democracia bárbara (Mexico: A
Barbarous Democracy), 1958, and Ensayo sobre un
proletariado sin cabeza (Essay Concerning a
Headless Proletariat), 1962. Thus Revueltas soon
emerged as a major political theoretician.

With the publication of his sixth novel, Los
errores (Errors), in 1964, Revueltas rendered into
fiction his many years of battles and frustrations
with the Mexican Communist party. Errors was to
be his final statement of the Mexican Communist

party and its failure to represent the masses. Aside from several short stories, it was the last fiction he would write for another five years. In 1965, he wrote El conocimiento cinematográfico y sus problemas (Theory and Problems of Film), a product of his many years in Mexican cinema. Although after 1965 Revueltas virtually retreated from writing fiction, he did receive major recognition as an artist in 1967 with the appearance of his Obra literaria (Literary Works), for which he received the Xavier Villaurrutia Literary Prize.[20]

Tlatelolco and Its Aftermath, 1968-1976

If Revueltas's life had been in relative limbo for a number of years, his situation was about to change dramatically, for in 1968 the long established political and social warrior was to experience a dramatic historical event in which he would be a major figure. In February 1968, Revueltas was invited to Cuba as a member of the literary jury for the Casa de las Américas. Since he was now an employee of the Secretary of Public Education, he was advised by his government not to travel to Cuba. Ignoring government threats, Revueltas travelled to Havana and, upon returning, publicly renounced his government job after an apparent attempt was made to punish him by freezing his salary.

Mexico City was preparing for the Olympic Games with great enthusiasm. At the same time, a host of radical Mexican groups, primarily students, were organizing for massive protests. Realizing that the eyes of the world would be upon

Mexico during the Olympiad, the students hoped to draw attention to their country's grave economic and political problems. Revueltas actively participated in numerous meetings and seminars held throughout the city. In addition, he authored and helped edit numerous pamphlets and circulars positing the Student Movement's concerns and demands. Somewhat spontaneously he emerged as a leading figure throughout several months in the summer and fall of 1968. On the evening of 2 October, after more than two months of confrontations, a mass student demonstration in the Plaza de Tlatelolco ended with a bloody government attack upon the demonstrators, leaving a large number of dead and wounded.[21] Revueltas, a prominent intellectual leader in the Student Movement, along with many other professors and students, was rigourously sought by the police. To avoid capture, Revueltas went "underground" for six weeks, being carefully hidden in Mexico City. On 16 November he was arrested, taken to an unspecified locale, and held captive for several days. During that time he dictated to the police a long statement in which he essentially confessed both to having been the leader of the Movement and to having committed specific crimes. On 22 November he was formally charged with ten criminal acts and remanded to Lecumberri Prison to await trial.[22] Initially he was carefully isolated from his fellow intellectuals and students within the prison, but after a threatened hunger strike he was quickly moved to the cell block containing his cohorts. Revueltas's trial was delayed until 17-18 September 1970. On 12 November, almost two years after his arrest, he was sentenced to sixteen years' imprisonment in Lecumberri.

Revueltas's last imprisonment was particularly hard on him physically, and it undoubtedly played a role in his early death. Various hunger strikes aggravated his diabetic condition. The political prisoners were often harassed by common prisoners. Of special importance was New Year's day, 1970, when students and professors were assaulted by other inmates, apparently with the full knowledge of prison officials.[23] In addition to the psychological and physical duress of prison life, Revueltas's wife, María Retes, divorced him during his stay in Lecumberri. Photos comparing the author immediately prior to entering Lecumberri Prison and others taken shortly after his release in May 1971 reveal the startling physical effects of imprisonment. Nevertheless, Revueltas managed to stay busy writing while in confinement. He produced a number of excellent short stories and a short novel titled El apando (Isolation Cell).

Ironically, Revueltas's release from Lecumberri came about as a result of President Echeverría's decision to release the parties charged with involvement in the Student Movement of 1968. Echeverría had been active in the pursuit and prosecution of the demonstrators as a government official during the Díaz Ordaz presidency. It is important to note, though, that the accused prisoners were not pardoned, but simply released with the vague promise of having their cases considered at a future date.

Now in ill health, Revueltas was once again given a position with the National Cinematographic Bank. In 1972 he traveled to Stanford University in California as a visiting lecturer. While there he met his last wife, Ema Barrón, whom he married in 1973. Returning to Mexico City, Revueltas occupied himself with writing and lecturing. In

1974 his third collection of short stories, Material
de los sueños (Dream Matter), appeared. One year
later, President Echeverría undertook a world-wide
tour of the Third World nations, including Cuba.
Perhaps as a gesture to Fidel Castro, Echeverría
included both Revueltas and Juan Rulfo in the
presidential entourage, since both men were
esteemed by the political left in Mexico. The
invitation to travel to Cuba under such
circumstances was initially rejected by Revueltas,
for obvious political reasons. He judged it unwise
to associate himself officially with the Mexican
government. Finally, though, he relented because
he wanted to see his Cuban daughter, whom he had
not seen since 1968. Revueltas clearly saw the
irony involved. It had been his insistence, in 1968,
to travel to Cuba that had precipitated his trouble
with the Mexican government. Now he was
returning to Havana as an official member of his
government's delegation.

Upon his return to Mexico City, plans were
prepared to perform his play Pito Pérez en la
hoguera (Pito Pérez in a Fix), originally written in
the 1950s. Revueltas took great interest in the
production of the play, which debuted in August
1975. It was to be the last personal literary event
in his lifetime. José Revueltas died in Mexico
City of a heart attack on 14 April, 1976. His
body was taken to the National University where
numerous eulogies were delivered. He was buried
the following day at the Panteón Francés de la
Piedad. The burial ceremony, in many ways, was
ironically representative of his life. During the
graveside gathering, student radicals shouted down
a government official who was attempting to
eulogize the author; order was established after
many threats and insults were exchanged. Mexico

City newspapers gave front-page coverage to the event, in a tribute to one of Mexico's greatest writers and intellectuals. Given his disdain for material wealth, it is not surprising that Revueltas died penniless. His funeral and hospital bills were paid by the Cinematographic Bank, his longtime employer. At the time of his death, Revueltas was putting in order his many political writings, which were to be part of an all-inclusive series of his literature, both published and unpublished. He left two unfinished novels, Hégel y yo (Hegel and I) and El tiempo y el número (Time and Number).

Apart from the purely factual data concerning Revueltas's life, there remains a residual image of the man in Mexico. To this day he is a symbol of intelligence and purity for many university students, artists, intellectuals, and political activists. For some, his life was exemplary of the highest idealism. On the other hand, he remains a symbol of misguided radicalism and inveterate hostility for the "old guard" of Mexican politics and society. Few Mexicans familiar with Revueltas's life react dispassionately to his name. Whatever the case, however, José Revueltas's life was unquestionably a testament to the common man. Whether or not one impugns his politics, his motives were genuine and his life was illustrative of selflessness, generosity, and a love for the Mexican people. Above all, his actions were thoroughly consistent with his political and social ideals, a fact seldom witnessed in the panorama of Latin American literature.

On a personal level, Revueltas is remembered for his humor, love of family, willingness to endure hardship, and boundless energy. If he were, at times, naive in judgment, or unduly pugnacious, his courage and sincerity counterbalanced these defects of commitment.

Chapter Two

The Novels

Although he wrote numerous volumes of short stories, plays, and essays, José Revueltas is most remembered as a novelist. This reputation is based upon the seven novels he produced during his distinguished literary career: Los muros de agua (Walls of Water), El luto humano (The Stone Knife), Los días terrenales (Earthly Days), En algún valle de lágrimas (In Some Valley of Tears), Los motivos de Caín (The Motives of Cain), Los errores (Errors), and El apando (Isolation Cell). A survey of these novels reveals works of varying lengths and quality; but taken as a whole, Revueltas's novelistic efforts must be considered to be of capital importance in the formation of the Mexican novel in the twentieth century. Along with Agustín Yáñez and Juan Rulfo, Revueltas is often viewed today as a founding father of the contemporary Mexican novel.

Full appreciation of Revueltas's seminal role in the creation of Mexico's "new narrative" was slow to develop. Only in recent years has he been widely acclaimed as a master novelist and literary innovator. Prior to the 1960s, mention of Revueltas's novels in literary histories was appallingly brief and incomplete. His works and influence were conveniently relegated to a minor position in standard reference books. Revueltas was often described as "honest," "interesting," or "promising," yet his significance was overlooked. The development of Mexican narrative from its basic Novel of the Revolution to the more sophisticated and experimental works of Yañez, Rulfo, Arreola, and others, was often portrayed as a quantum leap, without the direct participation of Revueltas.

Increasingly, however, critics and scholars recognize Revueltas as a major force in the creation of Mexico's contemporary novel and short story. José Alvarado, for example, observes that Revueltas produced "the first distinct and original narrative expression since the works of Martín Guzmán and Mariano Azuela. . . ."[1] Luis Leal has suggested that without the literature of Efrén Hernández and Revueltas, the works of better-known authors such as Agustín Yañez and Juan Rulfo "cannot be explained satisfactorily."[2] Thus, a slow but persistent reevaluation of Revueltas's importance to the contemporary Mexican novel during the last ten years continues to elevate his stature as a novelist.

To comprehend and appreciate Revueltas's novels, various historical, political and literary factors must be taken into account. The author's adult life spanned some five decades and was witness to a dynamic and unstable national development. During this period Mexico and her people struggled to consolidate the Revolution and simultaneously deal with massive problems of illiteracy, poverty, unemployment, and a host of other social ills. Revueltas actively participated in his nation's history and politics, involving himself in political parties, radical movements, labor strikes, and student demonstrations. Unlike many Latin American writers who proudly proclaim their leftist political sympathies from the comfort of their living rooms, Revueltas was a fully certified Marxist revolutionary who possessed an intimate, firsthand knowledge of Mexico's marginal leftist movements—their hopes, fears, and aspirations. His total commitment to a Marxist-Leninist idealism was reflected in a major way through his novels; strong autobiographical currents pervade the works, producing an ever-present sense of Mexican history and politics which, although fictionalized, has historical fact as its substratum. Thus history itself assumes a key function in unlocking the secrets of Revueltas's novels.

Closely allied with the issue of history is the question of politics. As Revueltas's close friend and comrade Eduardo Lizalde observes, "nothing will be understood of Revueltas's work if one does not penetrate in depth that political passion which completely defines him."[3] Unfortunately, Lizalde's observation has seldom been taken seriously by scholars. Instead of fruitfully investigating Revueltas's complex political career, which informs the very content of his novels, many students have earnestly chased myth and symbols while avoiding the intentional (political) focus of the author.

In contrast to his short stories, the novels are noteworthy for their political content. The fact that Revueltas utilized his novels for the formation of major political statements is complicated by the whole issue of Communist party dogma as it relates to literary theory. While no attempt is made in this study to investigate the intriguing and confusing questions pertaining to Communist writers in Latin America from the 1930s to the 1950s, a few general comments are in order. Further discussion is undertaken in Chapter 5—The Essays.

Revueltas was extremely interested in literary criticism and theory. He never relented in his efforts to reconcile the questions of realism, alienation, and class consciousness in literature. It was in the novels that Revueltas was most concerned with the problems of literature, society, socialism, and the artist. These preoccupations, in turn, were generated from his political orientation and affiliations with the Mexican Communist party. Specifically, Revueltas, like many Marxist writers in Latin America and throughout the world, struggled with the issue of Socialist Realism and the Communist party's right to dictate literary policy and to censure Party members.[4] This fundamental problem was central to much of Revueltas's literature until 1960, when he suffered his last expulsion from the Party. Most of his novels prior to that date exhibit a clear intent to reject Party literary dogma, although there are notable exceptions to the contrary. As Revueltas pursued an unorthodox position in both literature and politics, he fell prey to attacks from fellow Marxist writers and colleagues. He was accused of adopting and promoting Sartrean existentialism, a favorite accusation used by Marxist leaders in the 1940s and 1950s to control and intimidate Party artists. Although he was essentially ordered to denounce existentialism as an acceptable philosophy, his literature developed otherwise, much to the consternation of his friends.[5] Revueltas appeared to be attempting a synthesis of Marxism and an ill-defined existentialism. There are multiple parallels between Revueltas's philosophic development and the emergence of an existential Marxism in Europe.

Revueltas's intensely political nature, then, in unison with the historical period in which he lived, provides perhaps the most important aperture to a study of his novels. His daughter Andrea has observed, "Any aspect of my father's life that one studies will be allied with his fundamental passion, the revolutionary struggle for the transformation of the world in which we live, the struggle for Socialism. . . ."[6] This basic political concern manifested itself concretely in history and, hence, in his novels. To understand Revueltas's novels is to understand the governments of Calles and Cárdenas, the Stalinist Era, the Moscow Trials, and the Cold War, for as we shall see these events and a myriad of others surfaced directly and indirectly in the novels.

In addition to the historical and political axes, various literary influences played a role in the development of Revueltas's novels. He began his literary career at a time when Mexican narrative had reached a culminating point. By the late 1930s, two major schools of narrative had defined themselves in Mexico. Realism, primarily represented by the Novels of the Mexican Revolution, had become an established literary tradition. Writers such as Mariano Azuela, Martín Luis Guzmán, José Rubén Romero, and a host of others produced vividly realistic portraits of Mexico's violent revolution. By the 1930s, however, there emerged a small but influential group of authors who disavowed the purely external and descriptive Novels of the Revolution and began to cultivate a fresh narrative based on an interior, psychological view of man and his reality. Employing European models and techniques, writers such as Efrén Hernández offered a radically new alternative to the prolific realists who had inundated Mexico with action novels. The new "imaginative literature," as Emmanuel Carballo calls it, invited a marriage with Mexican Realism. Timothy Murad observes: "Their fusion took place in the literature of José Revueltas."[7] In the process of inheriting and melding these two diverse currents, Revueltas necessarily absorbed a variety

of Mexican and European influences. Like all
authors, he assimilated other writers' styles,
techniques, and themes in both conscious and
unconscious processes.

Since the issue of literary influences in
Revueltas's works is problematical, it is perhaps
most productive to cite those authors that
Revueltas himself considered to be either of capital
importance in his own formation as a writer, or at
least those authors whom he most admired. In
various interviews, Revueltas was repeatedly asked
to name such writers. Among the Mexican authors
most often mentioned were Mariano Azuela, Martín
Luis Guzmán, Juan de la Cabada, Efrén Hernández,
Heriberto Frías, and Angel de Campo. With regard
to European writers, Revueltas displayed a certain
fondness for the Russian masters, Dostoyevsky,
Tolstoy, and Chekhov. His list of favorites also
included Proust, Balzac, Malraux, Kafka, Sartre,
Solzhenitsyn, and Cervantes. This very eclectic list
points to the complexity of the question concerning
influence in Revueltas's works. The author himself
wavered on the issue. In 1967, when asked to
name the most important literary influences in his
work, Revueltas cited both Malraux and
Dostoyevsky.[8] Years later, when questioned by
Adolfo Ortega, Revueltas insisted that Proust was
the greatest influence in his work.[9]

One particular issue of literary influence that
has the proportions of a polemic must be
mentioned separately. For some two decades it
has been fashionable to note the strong presence of
Faulkner in Revueltas's early novels. The primary
source of this idea appears to be James Irby's "La
influencia de William Faulkner en cuatro narradores
hispanoamericanos."[10] Since Irby's study, numerous
critics, mostly Mexican, have almost casually

promoted this view. Emmanuel Carballo's belief
that Faulkner was Revueltas's "master" is typical.[11]
To be sure, there are various techniques commonly
associated with Faulkner that are also found in
Revueltas's novels, but their presence may be
either accidental or, at least, a result of indirect
sources. In any case, Revueltas vigorously denied
such influences. In 1962 he rejected Irby's
conclusion regarding Faulknerian influences and
insisted that prior to writing The Stone Knife he
had never read Faulkner.[12] Revueltas went on to
insist that apparent similarities between his works
and those of Faulkner were, unfortunately,
coincidental. In 1967, Revueltas stated his case
more succinctly: "When some critics have said
that Faulkner is my literary model, they are
wrong."[13] Arguing against the claim of
Faulknerian influences, various critics, including
José Agustín, have vigorously defended Revueltas's
position.[14]

The most often cited example of presumed
Faulknerian influence in Revueltas's novels centered
on the relationship between The Stone Knife and
Faulkner's As I Lay Dying. As early as 1943, José
Luis Martínez suggested that the similarities
between the two works were substantial.[15]
Although Martínez may have known the Faulkner
novel in its English version, Revueltas did not,
since his knowledge of English was virtually nil.
Interestingly, As I Lay Dying was not translated
into Spanish until 1942, the very year Revueltas
was completing The Stone Knife. That translation,
printed in Spain, may or may not have reached
Mexico prior to the publication of The Stone Knife.
At any rate, Revueltas's contact with As I Lay
Dying is problematical. Numerous other critics,
presumably as well read as Martínez, failed to note

the supposed similarities between the two works. In 1947, when the work appeared in the United States, North American critics made no mention of As I Lay Dying with respect to The Stone Knife. While general similarities may be conceded as a result of indirect contact, any notion that Revueltas conceived or executed The Stone Knife utilizing As I Lay Dying as a stylistic, technical, or thematic model must be challenged. On balance, Revueltas's argument of pure coincidence prevails as a plausible explanation.

One final observation must be made concerning the question of literary influences in Revueltas's novels. Complicating the issue is the fact that Revueltas was intensely interested in literary theory. Specifically, he was quite familiar with major Communist literary codes and theoreticians, from Gorki to Lukács. His desire to conform or not conform to Party philosophy and literary dogma often colored other influences. Thus, at times the reader suspects that the greatest literary influence present in Revueltas's novels is not that of a fellow novelist, but rather the persistent presence of a literary theoretician.

A number of generalizations can be made concerning both the thematics and characters with respect to the novels. Revueltas was preoccupied with the internal and external workings of the Communist party. He addressed such issues as alienation, the Party member's responsibility, history and class consciousness, human communication, class conflict, and Marxism versus existentialism. On a less abstract level are the recurrent themes of incarceration, sex, violence, death and the grotesque. This latter component, at times shocking and vulgar, was fundamental in Revueltas's portrayal of man's existential plight in the face of solitude, alienation, and oppression.

The majority of characters who populate the novels belong to the margins and lower strata of society. There is an abundance of Party workers, criminals, laborers, prostitutes, and prison guards. In contrast to the poor and disadvantaged is a small group of government officials, Party leaders, and members of the petite bourgeoisie, who represent negative symbols of power. Revueltas's characters often anguish in the midst of extreme life and death situations, desperately trying to resolve both physical and intellectual predicaments.

Walls of Water (1941)

Prior to the publication of Los muros de agua (Walls of Water), Revueltas had already published various short stories in Mexican literary journals. In addition, he had written, but not published, a short novel titled El quebranto (The Surrender). The manuscript unfortunately was stolen from him and, unwilling or unable to reconstruct it, he abandoned the project. A short version of the work, also titled "El quebranto," subsequently appeared in the short-story collection Dios en la tierra (God on Earth). Walls of Water, therefore, was Revueltas's first published novel. Its publication was financed by family and friends.

As Revueltas often explained, Walls of Water was an attempt to portray his personal experiences endured during two separate incarcerations in the infamous penal colony of the Islas Marías. These two imprisonments, one in 1932 for five months and another in 1934 for ten months, were the direct result of his political activities in association with the PCM. Significantly, the novel addresses

itself to a very real period in Mexican history.
The early 1930s witnessed a dogged effort by the
Mexican government to pursue and jail leftist
militants involved in labor union movements.   In
1961, upon the publication of the novel's second
edition, Revueltas wrote an introduction to the
work which served to explain and define the novel's
literary intent.   Accordingly, he argued that Walls
of Water was "like a tentative attempt"[16] to write
a work based upon a dialectical-materialist realism.
For Revueltas, this meant several things.   First, it
was a rejection of both Socialist Realism and
Critical Realism.   Second, it signified a deliberate
attempt to select essential components of reality
and, by presenting them in interplay, act out the
internal movement of history in Hegelian fashion.
In a somewhat dramatic manner he proclaimed that
this new realism was an approach that "no one has
attempted in Mexico for the simple reason that
there are no writers who are both dialectical and
materialist."[17]   By his own admission, the novel
failed to meet his stated objectives.
     To summarize Walls of Water is somewhat
difficult because of the many fragmented episodes
and flashbacks that are not closely related
contextually to each other.   The initial chapters
deal with the transport of over two hundred
prisoners to the Islas Marías, first by railroad cars
and then by ship.   By using a cinematographic
sweep technique, the reader is introduced to a
variety of prisoners, including the five Communist
políticos who represent the narrative's focal point.
From the very first page, a sense of fear and
confusion reigns.   After arriving at the penal
colony, the four male political prisoners, Marcos,
Ernesto, Santos and Prudencio, are sent to Arroyo
Hondo, a work camp.   Thus they are separated

from their female comrade, Rosario, who is
assigned to work as a servant for Subteniente
Smith, a vicious prison guard. Through a series of
flashbacks the reader learns of Rosario's traumatic
childhood, ill-fated love affair, and pregnancy.
Predictably Smith tries to rape her one night, but
she is saved by the timely intervention of Soledad,
a prostitute prisoner who has befriended her. The
incident results in the transferral of the two
women to Arroyo Hondo, where Rosario rejoins her
comrades, who love and admire her. Meanwhile,
the four políticos try desperately to adapt to the
cruelty and oppression in the camp. Prudencio, the
strongest physically, becomes deeply depressed and
attempts suicide. He fails, however, sustaining a
head injury that renders him mentally impaired.
Because they are feared and hated by the prison
guards and officials, the Communists are given
double work detail; it is clear that the políticos
are more despised than the ruthless criminals who
surround them.

Interspersed among the various experiences of
the políticos are numerous anecdotes relating the
activities of the common criminals. Several
memorable characters merit mention. El Miles, an
uncommonly strong and proud black man, befriends
the four Communists, helping them endure their
work and bolstering their morale. Almost
pathetically, El Miles attempts an escape by trying
to swim to the mainland. Ramón, one of the many
prisoners who is designated as a trustee to guard
the others, is the object of a flashback that
reaches the proportion of an intercalated short
story. Falsely accused of having seduced an
acquaintance's wife, he was pursued fanatically for
years until being forced to kill the husband.
Another flashback relates the strange case of

Alvaro Campos, sentenced to thirty years for murder.

Of the various episodes, one in particular stands out. Two trustees, Maciel and El Charro, had been rivals in the civilian world. The latter had humiliated the former by stealing his woman. An ironic twist of fate has placed them side by side again, now in the Islas Marías. Maciel, who has harbored deep resentment for years, is now prepared to exact retribution from El Charro. Their conflict occurs when El Charro presumably rapes and severely beats Marquesito, a wretched drug addict. Maciel takes advantage of his status as guard and punishes El Charro by beating him.

Maciel then decides to possess Rosario sexually. Soledad, her friend, naively tries to protect her by plotting fatally to infect Maciel with syphilis. She must first infect herself, however, by having intercourse with Temblorino, a miserable syphilitic. The novel concludes with the male Communist prisoners, as in the beginning, huddling together in face of overwhelming oppression. They are awaiting the arrival of their comrade, Rosario.

It is clear that Walls of Water both shocked and confused the literary critics. Viewed in conventional terms, the novel lacked formal structure and culmination. It might best be described as a loosely knit collection of anecdotes and situations held together by space and time. The successive experiences of the Communists, beginning with the land and sea voyages, and followed by their forced labor on the island, give the novel what little form and movement it possesses. While there is a general chronological time line, the temporal element is relegated to a level of virtually no importance. Little causality exists. Thus, the reader is often uncertain about the relationship of one event to another.

Of paramount importance in Walls of Water is the creation of a terrifying ambience that overwhelms the characters. One critic described the novel "as entering into death, into madness, into the enigma of outer darkness."[18] The reader is presented with an isolated and primitive island that is populated by Mexico's worst criminals and controlled by corrupt and sadistic officials. The prison work is arduous, disease is rampant, health facilities are almost nonexistent, punishment is severe, and escape is impossible. It is a world that assaults the mind and spirit and drives people to suicide, perversion, and incredibly inhuman acts. The effective portrayal of this inferno is effortlessly executed by Revueltas. The author claimed, however, that his true experiences in the Islas were worse than those depicted in Walls of Water.

There is a richness of characters in Walls of Water. A large gallery of rogues, misfits, homosexuals, prostitutes, and prison guards parades endlessly throughout the narrative. But there is little character description and development. Referring to Walls of Water, Emmanuel Carballo stated: "Revueltas almost never describes his characters physically. The reader imagines them through their actions."[19] Even in the case of the políticos, the object of the narration, the author does not permit them to assume specific personalities. The only exception is Rosario, who is portrayed as a beautiful and noble woman, full of strength and inspiration. Revueltas' elaboration of Rosario, while neglecting his other characters, however, appears to have no specific contextual significance.

The author does define the honorable in contrast

to the degenerate, though. Some guards are
seemingly compassionate, while others are vicious.
The reader is attracted to some prisoners and
repulsed by others. There emerges a dichotomy
between the Communists on the one hand and the
officials and guards on the other. The various
criminals, a large middle group, are designated as
either sympathetic or hostile to the políticos. In
the minimal characterizations, the line between
cruelty and compassion, reason and rage, and good
and evil is often obscured. Both prisoners and
guards seem to respond to primitive instincts and a
base desire simply to survive and to endure.

Particular mention must be made of the
políticos' function within the narrative. Imprisoned
solely for political reasons, they stand out amid the
population of common criminals. Although the
Communists exhibit great consternation and fear
when placed among the other prisoners, they
possess a bond of faith that transcends their
immediate reality. It is their common ideology and
comradeship—communism—that is their final refuge
of hope. If they are less prepared for hardships
experientially than the other convicts, they are
superior spiritually because of their politics. Even
though they suffer terrible abuses at the hands of
the blind and sadistic forces of corrupt prison
officials who represent an equally corrupt
government, the Communists somehow survive. In
spite of their idealism, however, the políticos are
not portrayed as purity and strength incarnate.
They do suffer, become confused, and gradually
evidence stress in the face of their environment.
Prudencio, for instance, collapses under the duress.
Rosario comes close to abandoning herself sexually
to El Charro. Ernesto and Marcos try to resolve a
petty jealousy concerning Rosario. The interjection

of five intelligent and civil young people amid Mexico's worst criminal element is, in the final analysis, a fascinating narrative pretext.

The language employed in Walls of Water provokes several key observations. An overview reveals that Revueltas's style is fundamentally conventional. Descriptive passages are basically denotative, although at times there is a surprising poetical sensitivity when describing the natural setting of the island, thus providing a sharp contrast to the glib, harsh, and realistic dialogues between prisoners. At times the reader perceives a kind of dialectic on a language level acted out between man and nature. A further observation concerns Revueltas's use of vulgarity, which he unabashedly cultivated in his literature to depict reality. In his first novels, such as Walls of Water, the use of such language shocked their readers. The provocative quality of his "Mexican crudity in spoken language"[20] progressively diminished, however, in the 1960s and 1970s as such language became commonplace in literature.

Walls of Water contains many of the recurrent themes to be found in Revueltas's subsequent novels: politics, alienation, Party affiliation, and the individual's quest for historical consciousness are all present. Sex, a thematic preoccupation of Revueltas, is treated in rather explicit terms--including both the pure and the perverse. Death, as man's constant companion, is basic to Walls of Water. As Prudencio, El Miles, and El Chale demonstrate, death represents the only escape from the Islas. The utilization of the grotesque as a fundamental aspect of man's existence is present in at least three markedly descriptive episodes: the battle of excrement waged by prisoners in the opening scenes, the

description of El Miles's mutilated body washed
ashore, and the syphilitic Temblorino.

Special mention must be made of incarceration,
which, in the opinion of many, was a trademark of
Revueltas. Perhaps more appropriately considered
as a personal metaphor, the subject of
imprisonment is not only a key to Revueltas's
entire novelistic corpus, but it is quite clearly the
very essence of Walls of Water. This theme, in
turn, abstracts into another, namely, alienation.
Treated in its most global sense, no one in Walls
of Water is immune to the ravages of alienation.
The Communists are as marginal to mainstream
Mexico as are the common criminals. The guards
and the officials mechanistically act out roles as
agents of a system that in no way integrates them
into a meaningful society. Rather, they are
seemingly recruited specifically because they are
dispensable. Perhaps the best example is the
grotesque Cuerpo Nacional de Inválidos, a pathetic
group of maimed soldiers in charge of moving the
prisoners around the island. The characters are
disconnected, but it is the resolution of this
alienation that Revueltas seems to seek out by
means of his dialectic in Walls of Water. Although
the novel is a direly pessimistic work, the end
contains a surprising element of hope. The
políticos, although totally intimidated by their
environment, nonetheless maintain hope for the
future. They sense that a new day will come, one
in which the organizing principles of society will be
radically transformed. In some undefined future
something "would rise up to liberate them."[21] The
final note of optimism is highly suggestive of
Socialist Realism and apparently was Revueltas's
concession to the Party's official literary dogma.

In spite of the fact that Walls of Water was

Revueltas's first published novel, it must be rated highly as a serious attempt at innovation and polished style. It remains, to this day, a convincing and poignant portrayal of injustice and human suffering. The autobiographical nature of the narrative seems to help rather than hinder the author's interpretation of this singular reality. Earlier accusations that the novel lacks structure and plot merit little consideration today. If there is fault to be found with the work it occurs when the omniscient narrator abruptly and awkwardly changes tone to editorialize politically. Fortunately, this seldom happens and thus does not seriously detract from the total narration. Walls of Water, therefore, must be judged as one of Revueltas's better novels. Most importantly, it contains many of the major themes and fictional personages that reappear in his subsequent works.

The Stone Knife (1943)

Winner of the 1943 Mexican National Prize for Literature, El luto humano (The Stone Knife) is undoubtedly Revueltas's most famous novel. It is, unfortunately, his only novel that has been translated to English, thanks to the work in 1947 by H.R. Hays.[22] Although certainly not his best novel from a technical standpoint, The Stone Knife catapulted Revueltas to instant literary fame in Mexico and earned him a permanent place of stature in that country's literature. While not all critics are in agreement as to the historical importance of The Stone Knife, many have emphasized the work's status as an initiator or point of departure for the contemporary Mexican novel. Luis Leal, for instance, considers it "the

first novel written by a Mexican author in which
an attempt is made to apply modern novelistic
techniques."[23]   While Leal's observation may be
somewhat overstated, The Stone Knife represented
a decisive and radically new approach to the
Mexican novel.   Timothy Murad insists that the
work "constitutes the first example of the nueva
novela in Mexico."[24]   Samuel O'Neill concludes that
The Stone Knife may properly be considered a
benchmark in Mexican literary history.[25]

The difference between The Stone Knife and
Walls of Water with regard to conception and
execution is colossal.   Whereas the latter was
loosely structured, employing essentially traditional
concepts of time and space, The Stone Knife was
tightly structured and employed numerous modern
narrative techniques: stream of consciousness,
mythic elements, fragmented time montage, and so
forth.   It was a clear attempt to construct a
highly sophisticated novel.   An analysis of the plot
leads one immediately into an intricate web of
flashbacks that take the forms of fleeting
memories, interpolated stories, and simple
anecdotes.   The reader is confronted with a maze
of juxtaposed time fragments that seek to create a
kind of cosmic, atemporal view of Mexico from the
pre-Columbian era to the Cárdenas presidency in
the 1930s.

The primary line of narration begins with the
death of Chonita, the infant daughter of Cecilia
and Ursulo.   The setting is their hut in a desolate
area of northern Mexico.   Cecilia sends her
husband to the nearby town to bring back the local
priest.   In Ursulo's journey to the church, however,
he becomes disoriented in a raging storm and
inadvertently stumbles upon the home of Adán, a
local henchman and assassin who at one time had

been under contract to kill Ursulo. Although apprehensive, Ursulo accepts Adán's offer to help him cross the swollen river to seek out the priest. While the two men return with the priest, Cecilia is visited by two couples who have come to mourn Chonita's death. Calixto and his wife, Calixta, and Jerónimo and his wife, Marcela, soon begin to drink tequila and become totally inebriated; their perceptions are blurred and they lose sense of time and space. Meanwhile, Ursulo and the priest arrive. Suddenly, Calixta inexplicably runs outside and disappears into the storm. She is the first to perish. The remaining men and women soon realize that they will all die in the rising waters from the nearby river.

A desperate evacuation begins in an attempt to avoid the flood. First Jerónimo drowns, and then the priest. The remaining members of the group wander aimlessly in the flood waters for an unspecified amount of time. They accidentally return to the hut and take refuge on the roof to await death. Three days pass while vultures circle above them. The novel ends with the party perishing in the raging waters.

The primary plot, although simple and chronological, serves as a pretext for a host of episodes related by flashbacks which are interrelated textually. Complementing and augmenting each other, these episodes produce a broad, rich vision of Mexico. Since Revueltas often embeds flashbacks within other flashbacks, the reader is forced to participate in the reconstruction of the historical time line. All action departs from the primary line of narration, a rather dreary story dealing with the attempt to escape the flood waters. But this is probably the least important part of the novel. It is, rather, the past and not the present which propels the narrative and engages the reader.

The immediate past deals with a workers' strike at the nearby Federal Irrigation System. Led by Natividad, a young Communist organizer, the workers had crippled the project until Natividad was murdered by Adán, the paid assassin. Ursulo had tried but failed to continue the strike. The figure of Natividad is reconstructed by both Ursulo and his wife, Cecilia, in numerous separate flashbacks. Natividad's personal story, in turn, generates a series of episodes including his various encounters with Adán, and his participation in the Mexican Revolution.

Among the more significant flashbacks are the priest's years as a seminarian and his subsequent experiences in the War of the Christers; the history of Ursulo's parents, culminating with the father's death in the Revolution; Calixto's participation in the Revolution, his encounter with Calixta, and their subsequent journey to Northern Mexico; and Adán's days as a cacique in a small village. In addition, there are numerous other fragments throughout the novel which echo Revueltas's search for the essence of the Mexican, his Revolution, and his history.

In The Stone Knife, Revueltas seeks to project a cosmic, ahistorical, totalizing vision of Mexico. Remarkably, the primary line of narration is locked very specifically in the modern history of Mexico. The real-life setting for the novel is an area near the town of Anáhuac in the northern portion of the state of Nuevo León. This region was the site of a large Mexican government irrigation system made possible by the construction of the Don Martín Dam on the Salado River. It was to this area that Revueltas went in 1934, under orders from the

Mexican Communist party, to organize a farm workers' strike. Thus, the immediate material for The Stone Knife comes directly from Revueltas's experiences as a labor organizer. The episodes treating the War of the Christers and the Mexican Revolution are also girded by an historical framework. Nevertheless, The Stone Knife reaches far beyond the concrete confines of the early twentieth century and moves backward in time, through references to the colonial period (Revueltas includes a documentary fragment from Father Sahagún) and into the mythic past of pre-Columbian Mexico. What begins as four desperate days in the lives of some Mexican peasants telescopes outward to a panoramic view of Mexico. Likewise, space in The Stone Knife expands from a purposely ill-defined area near the Don Martín Dam to a wide-ranging spatial treatment of Mexico, including Ciudad Juárez, Oaxaca, and Mexico City.

The psychological ambience of the novel is dense and brooding. There is an obvious and determined effort to immerse the characters in cataclysmic historical and natural forces which shape the psychology of the Mexican. Concretely, the primary line of narration reveals a sense of dire pessimism which is only resolved in death. The remaining poor peasants of the area act out a living hell of hunger and unemployment. Equally poignant are the disclosing episodes of the War of the Christers and the Mexican Revolution. Here Revueltas skillfully speaks to the confusion and corruption implicit in these two events. It is as if to live Mexico's history is to be contaminated spiritually and emotionally.

The Stone Knife is an investigation into the soul and psyche of the Mexican. The characters, taken as a whole, dramatically reveal the deep currents, both conscious and subconscious, of the Mexican's notion of self and reality. Ursulo, for example, mythically represents the modern vestige of Mexico's remote Indian past. Of humble means and capabilities, he is the enduring and suffering national bloodline. Full of contradictory qualities, he is acted upon, unable to reshape his destiny. He is a primitive mixture of conflicting emotions which reflects a childlike view of reality. While he loves Cecilia, his ultimate interest is one of possessing her sexually. His contradictory attitude toward Natividad was, on the one hand, that of boundless respect and undying loyalty. At the same time, however, he despised Natividad for the latter's many positive qualities.

One of the most interesting figures in The Stone Knife is the priest. Although in theory a spiritual leader, he has lost his faith and serves no useful purpose. Yet he continues to act out his role. He is, in short, the Mexican Catholic Church, morally and spiritually bankrupt. His one positive act in the novel occurs when he murders Adán, apparently as an afterthought, for the latter's violent crimes during the War of the Christers.

Adán, the paid assassin, is a violent and totally immoral creature who, although he shares the same bloodline with Ursulo, sells his services to the government and corporate interests of the ruling elite. He is, in the narrative context, that small but necessary portion of the Mexican populace (the army, police, informers) that permits the ruling classes to dominate the masses.

Certainly the central character in The Stone Knife is Natividad. In actuality the projected ego or alter ego of the author, Natividad is the Communist positive hero incarnate, full of strength, inspiration, courage, beauty, and intelligence. As such, he is Revueltas's major concession to Socialist Realism in the novel. The case of Natividad is an important one, for through his presence, action, and death the novel's message is propelled. Natividad had come to the region as a stranger. Soon he organized and led some five thousand peasants in a strike that paralyzed the government's irrigation project. He was virtually the only ray of hope in this dismal post-revolutionary Mexico. His physical death at the hands of Adán served only to elevate his stature in the eyes of his survivors. As Revueltas somewhat naively predicts, Mexico, one day, would be full of men like Natividad who would construct a new and vital country.

Finally, the women in The Stone Knife function as important secondary characters to flesh out the thoughts and personalities of their men. They are essentially submissive creatures whose plight is to suffer the indignities of a violent, male-oriented society. Unlike Walls of Water, in which Rosario acts out an important role, The Stone Knife has no truly substantial female characters.

The astonishing leap from the stylistically modest Walls of Water to the experimental narrative methods encountered in The Stone Knife suggests that Revueltas agglutinated most of the narrative innovations of the twentieth century within a mere two years in order to write his second novel. He brings to bear, at times with awkwardness, many devices generally not present in Mexican narrative in the early 1940s. Among the techniques employed, three merit special mention: interior monologue, fragmentation of time through flashbacks, and mythic components. From the first page of the novel, Revueltas launches a continual torrent of both direct and indirect interior

monologues to penetrate the psychology of his
characters. Preferring the more controllable
indirect monologue, Revueltas uses it to such an
extent that at times a kind of alternating game
appears between the omniscient narrator and the
monologues.

The manipulation of time is one of the salient
features of The Stone Knife. Through various
narrative techniques, Revueltas explores his
characters' pasts which form the novel's historical
superstructure. In the primary line of narration
Revueltas often plays with time by freezing action,
eliminating ordinary time markers such as night and
day, and generally confusing the reader as to
actual elapsed time. The past is fragmented by
flashbacks, some of which are embedded in other
flashbacks, to such a point that a reader only
knows he is in the historical past. The second half
of the novel consists almost entirely of episodes
related through flashbacks. Numerous other devices
are also used. O'Neill, in a detailed study of time
in The Stone Knife, has enumerated them: "motifs
and recurrence, circularism, simple and multiple
recollections, regression, preactive narration,
premonition, imaginative projection, interpolation,
paralysis, epiphany, dream and reverie, and
subjective perception."[26] But in spite of the
impressive list of devices employed to alter the
chronological time line, many are used with only
limited success. Some tend to muddle, rather than
enhance, the narration.

Critics have paid considerable attention to
mythic elements and structures in The Stone
Knife.[27] Revueltas develops two distinct mythic
strands: traditional Western Christianity and
indigenous mythology from both pre-Columbian and
Columbian Mexico. The author weaves and fuses

the two mythic strands to explore the internal contradictions in the Mexican spirit and psyche. The mixing of European and Indian mythic structures largely informs the characters' psychological and philosophical disarray.

Somewhat ironically, despite his Marxist convictions, Revueltas regularly used Christian myth, symbols, and concepts in his literature; he often employed these items in a demonic or inverted sense. Thus, in The Stone Knife Adán not only produces no progeny, but he is a bearer of death. Similarly, the exodus does not bring salvation, but a journey to death. Other identifiable Christian myths and symbols include the flood, the crucifixion, the Old Testament God, pervasive original sin, a Cain and Abel struggle, and the descent into hell.

Balanced against the many Christian references are many native Mexican myths of a primitive and telluric nature which speak to the questions of creation, purpose, and death. Connections are made between the elements of nature--animals, plants, and minerals—and man's spiritual-psychical state. Divine qualities are ascribed to the land. As an adjunct to this sort of animism, characters symbolically reflect nature. Thus, Cecilia, Antonia, and La Borrada are symbols of the land. Ursulo is the legendary "obsidian knife." The effect is to produce a formidable feast of mythic structures and symbols which intellectually entice the reader.

Many of the recurrent themes in Revueltas's novels are present in The Stone Knife. In his struggle to survive, man is placed in an extreme confrontation with reality, with no apparent escape. Alienation, solitude, and death are pervasive constants. As part of an elaborate existential portrayal of the Mexican, Revueltas merges historical, sociological, geographical, and political elements. But although The Stone Knife is immersed in an oppressive construct of pessimism and despair, the novel is, in fact, one of hope and promise. The constant presence of Natividad, the Socialist hero, points to a new day for Mexico. His physical death in no way detracts from the author's claim that the coming of communism to Mexico is inevitable, for as Revueltas observes, "Men like Natividad would rise up one morning over Mexico. New and with a smile. Then no one would be able to stop them because they would be the definitive enthusiasm and emotion."28 More than simply a sophisticated analysis of Mexican culture, The Stone Knife is a dramatic political statement of Mexico's future which would be guided and controlled by the Communist party.

Earthly Days (1949)

The Marxist idealism evident in both Walls of Water and The Stone Knife was totally congruent with Revueltas's politics during the first part of his literary career. With his expulsion from the Mexican Communist party in 1943, however, Revueltas's attitudes concerning the Party and revisionism began to take new directions. Although he was officially censured by the Communists, Revueltas remained loyal to both his Marxist ideals and his many Marxist colleagues. While he was considered a disruptive influence by Party officials, he enjoyed the admiration of many leftist intellectuals. His continual drift away from Party dogma, his flirtation with Lombardo Toledano's Popular party, and his calls for revisionism all contributed to a volatile denunciation of the Party which, in 1949, was contained in his third novel, Los días terrenales (Earthly Days). The work's polemical force initiated a political and literary controversy that raged in Mexico for many years.

The author's persona found in Earthly Days must be viewed within its own historical framework. Although in a planning stage for several years, the novel was published at the height of Stalinism and the "cult of personality." Revueltas, like so many Marxist artists during the 1940s, suffered a crisis of conscience when the crimes of Stalinism became self-evident. No longer able to remain silent on the matter, Revueltas attempted to transcend the problem by arguing for an essentially humanistic Marxism in Earthly Days. In doing so, he incurred the wrath of the Party and many of his friends.

Earthly Days consists of nine chapters, the first six of which are sequenced in a tripartite system so that the narrative moves among three distinct settings and points of view in a rotating fashion. Chapters 1 and 4 deal with Gregorio Saldívar, a young Communist organizer whom the Party has sent to Acayucan in the state of Veracruz; his objective is to organize the local fishermen into a cooperative. Although moderately successful in his efforts, Saldívar is censured and recalled by the Party for refusing to agitate against the local cacique, whom Saldívar considers to be a political progressive. In chapters 2 and 5 the setting moves to the Party's clandestine headquarters near Mexico City, where Fidel Serrano, a Party boss, and his wife Julia, live. The latter, an earnest and dedicated Party worker, is lamenting the death of the couple's infant daughter, Bandera. Fidel, an example of extreme Party loyalty and discipline, is more concerned with publishing the Party's newspaper than in attending to his child's funeral.

There develops a deep and irreconcilable conflict between Fidel and Julia which culminates in her decision to leave him. Chapters 3 and 6 are set in the outskirts of Mexico City, where two Party workers, Rosendo and Bautista, are making their way through the night toward an industrial sector of the city. Their objective is to disseminate Party propaganda. As they walk, the two men engage in a long discussion concerning Fidel and the Party.

Chapter 7, also set in Mexico City, takes place in the home of Jorge Ramos, an affluent architect who is also a Communist sympathizer. Much of the chapter is devoted to Ramos's sexual fantasies. Essentially a caricature of bourgeois morality and decadent life-style, Ramos offers his comfortable home to the Party for clandestine meetings. Chapter 8 moves to Puebla and a meeting between Gregorio and Fidel. The former had been ordered to Puebla to take charge of a hunger march of unemployed workers. Fidel has come to Puebla to outline the details of the march. During their discussion the two men argue solemnly over Party doctrine. The last part of the chapter describes, in vivid detail, Gregorio's visit to a health clinic to be treated for a venereal disease that he contracted in Acayucan. Chapter 9 occurs in a darkened prison cell occupied by Gregorio, who has been arrested for his participation in the hunger march. The reader is privy to a series of strange and dramatic visions imagined by the prisoner. The novel ends with Gregorio awaiting the arrival of prison guards who are coming to torture him.

As in most of Revueltas's novels, Earthly Days contains a rich variety of significant flashbacks which often reach the dimension and impact of a short story. In Chapter 3, for example, Bautista recalls with horror how Fidel had used the money intended for Bandera's funeral to prepare the Party's newspaper. In Chapter 5, Julia remembers her first encounter with Fidel and their subsequent marriage. Chapter 7 contains Ramos's detailed recollection of his affair with his mistress. In Chapter 8, Fidel recalls the Party meeting at Ramos's house and the accusations hurled against Gregorio.

Earthly Days is set concretely in Mexico's history and geography. Both the locales and time element correspond to Revueltas's early years as a Party labor organizer. This fact and others make Earthly Days, like Walls of Water and The Stone Knife, much more autobiographical than is readily apparent.[29] Earthly Days reflects Revueltas's political philosophy of the 1940s. The physical ambience effected in Earthly Days is varied and spatially wide-ranging. The action moves from the jungles of Veracruz to the suburbs of Mexico City to the streets of Puebla. Unlike Revueltas's earlier novels, Earthly Days has, in parts, an urban flavor. The narrator describes the older, less savory parts of Mexico City's north side, which contrasts sharply with the opulent apartment belonging to Ramos.

Of particular note is Revueltas's interlacing of spatial confinement to produce a hermetic and oppressing psychological environment. The opening scenes at night in the jungle near Acayucan, for example, describe Gregorio's awe when faced with the nocturnal powers of nature. No less intimidating is the small house where Fidel and Julia hide in constant fear of being discovered by the authorities. Rosendo and Bautista become disoriented both spatially and temporally in a Mexico City garbage dump. They are engulfed in a darkness that ravages their spirit. The sense of confinement approaches claustrophobia when the narrator describes Ramos's apartment. Yet the most devastating example of spatial limitation occurs at the end of the novel when Gregorio is imprisoned in a small cell without light. Suffering from virtual sensory isolation, he begins a series of surreal visions that border on hallucinations. In short, the psychological ambience, shaped strongly by confinement, projects various scenes of stress, confusion and impending terror.

Characters, rather than action, inform the central material of Earthly Days. The novel's primary development centers on a clash of personality and ideology between Gregorio Saldívar and his Party boss, Fidel Serrano. The former (clearly Revueltas's persona) is portrayed as a thoughtful and warm human being who seriously questions the wisdom of Party doctrine. Although he is a loyal Party worker, he is also capable of doubting and even defying his Party's judgment and methods of operation. Fidel, on the other hand, is an inflexible, myopic Party functionary whose strict and unquestioning adherence to dogma is unmatched. Totally dedicated to the Communist cause, his zeal has utterly dehumanized him. Both Gregorio and Fidel are explicit in their denunciation of one another. Whereas Fidel brands his one-time friend as a "petit bourgeois,"[30] Gregorio considers his boss to be nothing more than "a scheme, a deformed phenomenon, a spiritual schematicism."[31] Fidel blames Gregorio's political heresy on his intellectual background. Gregorio observes that Fidel's lack of human understanding is the result of his ascendancy in the Party's hierarchy. As Jaime Labastida states, the two men are "the antagonic incarnations of two ways of assuming Communism and its morality."32 The central female character in <u>Earthly Days</u> is Julia. She had married Fidel after her true love, Santos Pérez, had been assassinated. Although Julia's husband is obsessed with her, his politics have so robbed him of emotion that he cannot express his love for her. Julia progressively begins to echo Gregorio's opinion of her husband. She comes to believe that Fidel "is sordid, empty and cold inside."33 At the same time, she cannot hate him because she realizes that he is sincere and useful to the Party's causes.

Two other characters, Bautista, and Rosendo, make up the cast of principals in <u>Earthly Days</u>. Both loyal Party workers, they debate and ponder the case of Fidel. The younger, more idealistic Rosendo views Fidel as the very model of the exemplary Communist leader. The older and more experienced Bautista, on the other hand, shares Gregorio's negative assessment of Fidel. Rosendo is shocked when Bautista reproaches him for the gratuitous compliments that he heaps upon Fidel. In short, the function of Bautista and Rosendo is to elaborate in more objective terms the philosophical dichotomy represented in the conflict between Gregorio and Fidel.

One character, Jorge Ramos, deserves special mention. Although not an integral part of the central material, Ramos assumes prominence in the narrative as the only substantial counterpoint to the large cast of Party workers. Revueltas's tremendous powers of characterization are at their best when portraying Ramos as a neurotic intellectual whose superficial existence is a quagmire of deception, repression, and self-indulgence. The devastating portrait of Mexico's bourgeoisie, as viewed in Ramos, leaves no doubt as to Revueltas's ultimate class loyalties.

Earthly Days contains many interesting secondary characters. In Acayucan, Gregorio works with Tuerto Ventura, an imposing village leader. In flashbacks we meet Epifania, a local woman who, because of her love for Gregorio, kills Macario Mendoza, the local head of the government's White Guard. Mendoza, apparently intent upon killing Gregorio, is reminiscent of Adán in The Stone Knife. The episode with Jorge Ramos introduces his wife, Virginia, and his mistress Luisa, both of whom are the decadent female counterparts of Ramos. The lowest level of the Party's hierarchy is portrayed by Ciudad Juárez, an old and feeble Party aid, while the highest level of Party officials appears in the person of Bordes, the head of the Central Committee.

The language and stylistic techniques found in Walls of Water and The Stone Knife are essentially those employed in Earthly Days. The latter work, however, shows more narrative control. The manipulation of time, multiple point of view, indirect interior monologues, biblical language and symbols, myth, discursive digressions, and poetical language are all used with more prudence. Whereas at times The Stone Knife displays an awkward restructuring of the temporal element, Earthly Days moves effortlessly backward and forward in time. Nor are the flashbacks as gratuitous as in the earlier novels. Rather, they serve as substantial ligatures that bind the action and material of the various chapters. The transitions from the primary line of narration to flashback episodes are smoother and less obvious. All things considered, Earthly Days is stylistically superior to both Walls of Water and The Stone Knife.

There are a number of minor but impressive stylistic touches not present in the earlier works. One such item occurs in Chapter 2 when the action is marked by the passage of minutes on the face of a clock. Another occurs when Bautista and Rosendo walk on the outskirts of Mexico City. Here Revueltas momentarily merges visions of pre-Columbian Tenochtitlán with the sounds of the modern city, all of which is achieved through a powerful lyricism. Also of interest is Gregorio's scientific and anatomical treatment of his impressions of Macario Mendoza's cadaver.

Perhaps the greatest stylistic accomplishment to be found in Earthly Days occurs in the last chapter when Gregorio, suffering from sensory isolation, torture, and disease, enters a nearly surreal plane and speculates on life, death, love and sex. At one point he imagines himself exploring the interior of his mother's womb. To achieve this startling and spectacular ending for the novel, Revueltas limits his character's physical reality to only the tactile. This, in turn, unleashes Gregorio's mental faculties, resulting in a barrage of strange and frightening visions. The author uses a brilliant combination of poetical, biblical, philosophical, scientific, mathematical, and ethical language to project the episode.

It is not the narrative style and technique, however, but rather the philosophical and political content of Earthly Days that is very new and different—so much so that the 1949 work reveals a vastly changed author from that of the early 1940s. These changes converge and express themselves in essentially two principal themes: existentialism and revisionism. Virtually all other themes in Earthly Days serve to define and extend the two primary topics.

Beginning with his opening paragraph, Revueltas suggests an existential direction for Earthly Days: "In the beginning there had been Chaos, but suddenly that lacerating magic spell dissipated and life began. Atrocious human life."[34] From that point forth the novel posits numerous existentialist tenets: the absense of absolutes in life, the hopelessness of human existence, the anguish of knowledge, and man's solitude and alienation, to name but a few. These ideas, so antithetical to the confidence and promise of Marxism, emphasized a loss of faith on Revueltas's part. Thus, unlike the enthusiastic and optimistic Natividad in The Stone Knife or the confident políticos in Walls of Water, Gregorio is completely demoralized and awaits further torture at the end of Earthly Days. In short, the Communist hero has lost hope in the future and, hence, in man. Even in conceding the eventual triumph of communism, Gregorio asserts that man himself will not change.

The somewhat less philosophical, but more condemnatory theme of revisionism occupies the spotlight with existentialism in Earthly Days. Revueltas concretely and specifically accuses the Communist party of blind and dogmatic behavior that alienates not only the people, but its own workers. This anti-Party position is devastatingly persistent throughout the narrative. The Party's hierarchy is repeatedly likened to that of the Catholic Church, where zeal and blind discipline rule over reason. The Party, personified and symbolized in the person of Fidel, assumes a negative, dehumanizing posture in the historical process, completely contrary to its avowed function.

Subsumed by existentialism and revisionism are a variety of recurrent themes. Sex and sexuality, for example, are present throughout the novel, ranging from Fidel's compulsive sexual possessiveness of Julia to Ramos's erotic fantasies to Gregorio's sexual encounter with Epifania. Death is treated in numerous instances and manners, most notably in the cases of Macario Mendoza and Bandera (the latter being reminiscent of Chonita in The Stone Knife). Incarceration appears as a major component of Earthly Days at the end of the novel. The author's penchant for the grotesque is disclosed in the death of Macario Mendoza, and above all in the graphic description of Gregorio receiving treatment for a venereal disease.

The publication of Earthly Days in 1949 provoked a literary and philosophical polemic that ended with Revueltas's denunciation and voluntary withdrawal of the novel in June 1950 (see discussion of Quadrant of Solitude in Chapter 4). This singular episode in Mexican letters stands, to this day, as one of the most amazing events in Latin American literary history. The polemic was already in evidence in an article by Antonio Prieto in November 1949. After alluding to the criticism circulating in literary circles, Prieto attempted to defend and excuse Revueltas for having promoted existentialism; he openly disassociated Revueltas from the existentialists: "Revueltas does not belong to that crowd of desperate men without hope. His entire life has been a constant affirmation."[35] Prieto went on to place great faith in Revueltas as a star that had temporarily dimmed, but that would once again light up brilliantly and produce the great Mexican novel.

There followed various critiques of Earthly Days, both positive and negative, throughout the winter of 1949 and the spring of 1950. Central to the criticisms was the issue of existentialism. Undoubtedly, the critics sympathetic to the Communist party were more concerned with the novel's political content. Yet they tended to avoid the issue, since to attack Revueltas's anti-Party position would have appeared self-serving.

On 26 April 1950 Enrique Ramírez y Ramírez published a complete and total critique of Earthly Days in which he denounced the work as existentialist propaganda.36 It was not until two weeks later, with the debut of the play Quadrant of Solitude, that the polemic surrounding Earthly Days reached extraordinary intensity. From that point on, the fate of the novel and the play were inseparable. Some critics attacked one work, but not the other, while other critics attacked both simultaneously. Typical of the criticism launched against Earthly Days was that of Raúl González García: "The plot, characters, and dialogues are nothing but the author's fling with imported Sartreanism, a lack of merit and originality."37

It was Ramírez y Ramírez, however, who apparently sealed the fate of Earthly Days. His critique of the novel, made in April, was reprinted in a three-part series beginning on 11 June in El Nacional.38 The first part appeared the same day as Juan Almagre's response to Revueltas's response to Almagre's critique of Quadrant of Solitude (See Chapter 4). Ramírez's critique was uncompromising. He attacked Earthly Days with great vigor, and five days later, on 16 June, Revueltas published a public denunciation of his two works (see Chapter 4). Thus, one of the strangest episodes in Latin American literature had come to an end. In spite of Revueltas's public recanting, however, the remaining two Ramírez installments appeared in El Nacional during the subsequent weeks.

Ramírez's article, "Sobre una literatura de extravío," is important not only because it is one of the most thorough examinations of existentialism in Earthly Days, but particularly because it is an excellent example of Marxist criticism in the Stalinist era. Ramírez attacked the style, structure, message, and purpose of the novel. Pointing to its tendentiousness, he observed: "It's almost not a novel, but a pamphlet."[39] He insisted that Revueltas "preaches the blindness and impotence of man in the face of universal and social reality. . . ."[40] Ramírez's central theme, though, was existentialism: "It is impossible to read Earthly Days without bringing immediately to mind that pseudophilosophy and semiliterature that the pedants call 'existential philosophy.'"[41]

Although Revueltas publicly confessed to having erred in his approach to art and voluntarily withdrew his works (see discussion of Quadrant of Solitude in Chapter 4), in order to put an end to the polemic, he made numerous other public statements concerning his position with respect to existentialism, and specifically with regard to the content of Earthly Days. As early as mid-1949, shortly before the publication of Earthly Days, he spoke out sharply against existentialism in an interview in Novedades.[42] In May 1950, with special reference to Earthly Days, he insisted that he neither subscribed to existentialism nor intended Earthly Days to be a critique of the Mexican Communist party.[43] Six years later, in 1956, Revueltas spoke at length with Mauricio de la Selva concerning the denunciation of Earthly Days. In that interview Revueltas observed: "Earthly Days has as its point of departure a negative, antidialectical, and anti-Marxist consideration which is that of considering man as a being without any purpose on Earth."44   Revueltas went on to elaborate, however, that any suggestion that he was an existentialist was utterly false.

In 1962 Revueltas responded to a series of questions presented to him by the Mexican critic Luis Mario Schneider. His response appeared in El Día. Interestingly, Revueltas had softened his position of self-criticism: "I am inclined to consider Earthly Days my most mature novel."45   He once again insisted that the novel in no way criticized the Party's doctrine or communism in general. Rather, he argued that the Mexican Communist party did not exist in a true historical sense. Thus, any attack upon the Mexican Party in no way suggested an attack on the larger movement or doctrine of communism. He also refuted, once more, the charges that branded him as an existentialist.

Whether Revueltas's assimilation of generalized existentialist tendencies during the 1940s was done consciously or unconsciously will never be ascertained. Nevertheless, there is no question that the content of Earthly Days mirrors the mainstream of existentialist thought during that period. With respect to revisionism, the most torpid of interpretations clearly reveals Revueltas's intention to mount a frontal attack upon the Party. But, quite aside from these polemics, Earthly Days is one of Revueltas's better novels.

In Some Valley of Tears (1956)

With the death of Stalin in 1953, international communism took on new dimensions of hope for many Marxist artists who had either been expelled from the Party or had voluntarily withdrawn from its ranks. Stalin's death signaled the end of the so-called "Zhadnov era," which had represented total control of Communist writers for some eight years. With the ensuing "thaw" and the newly recaptured glamour of international communism as a practical political strategy, Revueltas was deeply moved; he formally sought readmission to the Mexican Communist party in early 1955. Prior to that, he wrote his fourth novel, En algún valle de lágrimas (In Some Valley of Tears), which he finished in December 1954.[46] His decision not to publish it until 1956 was most likely related to his uncertainty about his future relations with the Party and the tentative nature of the literary thaw.

Noteworthy in In Some Valley of Tears is the absence of Party politics and political references. At the same time, however, in conjunction and harmony with the Socialist Realism of the period, it was a brutal denunciation of Mexico's capitalistic society and its attendant social alienation. Thus, in general terms, it fulfilled the Party's literary credo. Because of the clear class distinctions and proper rendering of culpability, the work undoubtedly met with favor among Marxist critics.

The primary plot of Valley of Tears is the simplest to be found among Revueltas's seven novels; it relates the routine activities of a typical day in the life of a bourgeois landowner. Beginning with the protagonist's first waking moments, the action moves slowly and meticulously from bed to bathroom. After attending to bodily functions, he returns to the bedroom, where his housekeeper, Macedonia, helps him with his clothes as he carefully dresses and prepares to meet the day. He then leaves his house and sets forth to

accomplish two tasks: he must first consult with a
curandero about neutering his pet cat and then go
to collect overdue rent from his tenants.   As he
goes down the street of a commercial area, he
stops briefly at a church.   Upon returning to the
street, he stops to offer money to some poor
Indians.   On his way to see the curandero, he
suddenly spies his former school principal.   Passing
the man by, the protagonist stumbles upon a
raucous scene in which a laborer is killing a cat
suspected of rabies.   Suddenly remembering that his
own cat had bitten him several days earlier, the
landowner is struck with panic, fearing a case of
rabies.   He hurriedly heads back toward his doctor's
house.   When he once again passes the school
principal, the latter attempts to talk to him,
believing the protagonist to be someone he had
known in prison.   The startled landowner feigns
total ignorance and hurries on, disappearing into a
crowd on the street of the coffin makers,
whereupon the novel ends.

Interlaced throughout the novel are numerous
flashback episodes which relate significant events in
the protagonist's life.   Serving to elucidate the
perverse nature and personality of the avaricious
landowner, the scenes are evoked through various
devices of free association.   Many episodes center
on the landowner's schooldays as a young boy--his
friends, his teachers, the principal, and, above all,
the students' curious custom of going to a flea
market where they stare at a preserved human
fetus on display in a window.   This latter
experience has permanently crippled the
protagonist's attitude toward sex and progeny.   So
desperately does he fear offspring that when his
cat unexpectedly gives birth to a litter of kittens
the twisted protagonist, in a rage, flushes them

down the toilet as punishment for his cat. Aside from the preserved fetus, the most prominent and recurring memory from his school days is his winning of the school's monthly virtue awards. Twice he was honored, once for Truth and once for Fairness, two qualities conspicuously absent in the landowner's moral makeup. Various other flashbacks flesh out either the landowner's sexuality or his bourgeois materialism. He recalls a visit to a local house of prostitution; his repeated attempts to seduce his former fiancée; the death of his only friend, who had committed suicide over a business failure; and the manner in which he had saved his lawyer from prison by forcing him into bankruptcy and assuming ownership of the lawyer's personal belongings.

Valley of Tears is noticeably limited both spatially and temporally. The plot's action is confined to the interior of the protagonist's house and several streets in an unspecified city, presumably Mexico City. Even the flashbacks, also in unspecified locales, add little to spatial dimensions—a school, a flea market, a whore house, and an office. There is a clear attempt by Revueltas to create an hermetic, asphyxiating atmosphere that is the personal domain of the perverse landowner. In the case of the house and the street scenes, the author relies on careful description to suggest a sanctuary (the house) and a maelstrom of confusion and noise (the street). The primary line of narration occurs in some four or five hours, while the flashbacks extend backward in time some forty-five years. Noteworthy is Revueltas's ability to slow the passage of time to such a point that the reader senses minutes and even seconds. The protagonist's very concern with the passage of life, coupled with a morbid fascination with death, enhances the sharp contrast attained between the landowner's vacuous current existence and his curious nostalgia for the past.

The lyricism evidenced in the first three novels is noticeably absent in Valley of Tears. Revueltas turns to a biting realism that is uncompromising in both description and narrative material. The protagonist's visit to the toilet, including his struggle with intestinal problems and eventual bowel movement, is narrated with painstaking realism. In both description and characterization, Revueltas presents a grotesque but realistic portrait.

In spite of being a minor work in Revueltas's novelistic production, Valley of Tears is structurally one of his best novels. It suggests a clear intent on the author's part to "craft" a work that is internally harmonious. Relying on numerous devices of free association, flashbacks are evoked naturally and effortlessly. Utilizing indirect interior monologues, the deep recesses of the protagonist's mind slowly unfold. Revueltas works hard to distance himself from the narrator-protagonist, allowing authorial intervention only occasionally. Since the single point of view operating in the novel is that of the protagonist, the world-view afforded the reader is singular, cruel, and distorted. As the narrator-protagonist reveals his own self-delusion, prejudices, fears, hypochondria, and sexual disorientation, the reader apprehends the highly suspect point of view as presented by the unreliable narrator, who not only lies to others but to himself as well.

The only principal character in Valley of Tears is the elderly landowner, who is portrayed as a perverse, cruel, and materialistic symbol of the bourgeoisie. Revueltas deliciously reveals his many frailties and defects. The self-indulgent protagonist suffers from inordinately high self-esteem which so colors his personal image that he erroneously perceives his acts of avarice, deceit, and unfairness as virtuous. While he considers himself to be truthful and just (ironically, he had won the award for Truthfulness by lying), he lies without conscience and lacks any sense of justice. As a representative of the bourgeoisie, he engenders racial hatred and social prejudice. When a group of Indians appears in front of his house, for example, he is consumed with such disgust that he wishes that they would all die. His attitude toward Macedonia, a woman who generously cares for him, is one of disdain, as she is his social inferior. His tardiness in collecting rent from his tenants (due to his own forgetfulness) is construed as charity. In short, the landowner has no redeeming features. As Carlos Eduardo Turón has observed, the protagonist "has not the slightest notion of evil, in spite of the fact that he commits it with every pulse beat, with every breath."[47]

The very obvious absence of politics as a theme in Valley of Tears makes it unique among Revueltas's early novels, but many other recurrent themes are present in abundance. Both sex and death are centerpieces in the landowner's twisted existence. Class alienation and individual alienation pervade the novel. The protagonist's life is cast in solitude. Even a hint of incarceration appears in metaphoric form when, at the end of the novel, the landowner's former school principal announces: "We are all prisoners."[48] The extent to which this hapless ending may be interpreted as latent existentialism is speculative. What is certain is that there is no escape from this Valley of Tears. Revueltas readily indicts the bourgeoisie as the culpable party responsible for this sordid existence, but the author offers no promise of change or redemption. Hence, pessimism prevails in this world, devoid as it is of positive characters and positive symbols. The world of the landowner is nauseating and, as Jorge Ruffinelli observes, "the reader is intended to experience it."[49]

The Motives of Cain (1957)

Considered by most critics to be Revueltas's least impressive novel, Los motivos de Caín (The Motives of Cain) is the author's best example of a Socialist-Realist work. One year prior to its publication, Revueltas was readmitted to the Mexican Communist party. Once again free to publish as an orthodox Communist writer, he was cognizant of his colleagues' suspicions concerning his theoretical and practical literary views. Much had changed, however, since his problems with Earthly Days. With the initiation of Khrushchev's de-Stalinization programs and the ensuing relaxation of the Party's strict control over its writers, Revueltas gained newfound confidence as an artist.[50] Importantly, in 1954, the Second Congress of Soviet Writers was convened and a new definition of Socialist Realism was forged. This dramatic development was soon to afford Marxist writers the luxury of writing novels that, under the Stalinist era, would have been subjected to immediate censorship.

Revueltas went to the Soviet Union in 1957 to negotiate a film project. During his trip he apprised himself of the latest developments among Socialist writers, both inside and outside of the Soviet Union. That Revueltas was thoroughly conversant with the new Socialist aesthetics is evidenced by his activity in the essay during that period (see Chapter 5). Specifically, Realism in Art and an essay titled "A Letter from Budapest to Communist Writers" demonstrate that Revueltas was acutely aware of developing changes in Socialist Realism.[51] The new liberalization of the Socialist literary credo was undoubtedly received enthusiastically by Revueltas. Although the climate for Communist writers had changed greatly, the Mexican author was apparently reluctant to risk a renewed censure from his colleagues. Therefore, The Motives of Cain, not surprisingly, was congruent with the trendy winds of Socialist Realism of the period. It was a sound denunciation of North American imperialism, which was the surest way for a Marxist writer to prove his loyalty to the Communist cause during the post-Zhadnov era. But Revueltas went even further to avoid potential conflict with Communist critics by setting his novel, in large part, outside Mexico. By avoiding all mention of the Mexican Communist party, Revueltas removed from consideration any possibility of criticism from fellow Party members. For good measure, he inserted a positive hero into the novel to enhance the novel's conformity to Socialist Realism.

Motives consists of six chapters that treat three distinct episodes. Chapters 1 and 2 take place in the streets of Tijuana, Mexico. The narrator relates the aimless meanderings of Jack Mendoza, a Chicano military officer who has recently deserted from the United States Army and fled to Mexico. As he walks through the streets he is gripped with confusion, paranoia, and near delirium, having spent four days without sleep. Clearly an outsider, Mendoza fearfully observes Tijuana's inhabitants in pursuit of daily activities. The chapter ends with Mendoza recalling his desertion from the military base at San Diego.

Chapter 3 takes place in Los Angeles, some two weeks prior to his arrival in Tijuana. After deserting, Mendoza had gone to Los Angeles in search of his friends Bob and Marjorie Mascorro. Not finding them at home, he seeks refuge in their garage, where he is startled by the arrival of Lutero Smith, a deranged black Adventist minister. Smith informs him that there have been mass arrests of Chicanos following the death of a young boy. Smith concludes that Mendoza is responsible for the incident and suddenly runs away. The Mascorros, who are members of the Communist Party, arrive shortly thereafter and offer to help him escape across the border to Mexico.

In Chapter 4, the action shifts to Korea during the Korean war. Mendoza, an army sergeant, is on patrol with two soldiers. They chance upon Kim, a young North Korean who is covertly sending radio messages. After taking him prisoner, they escort him to their headquarters for interrogation. During their journey, Mendoza discovers that Kim, having been born to a Korean father and Mexican mother in Culiacán, understands Spanish. Jack, somewhat sympathetic toward the prisoner, fears that Kim will be taken as a spy instead of a common prisoner and thus will be mistreated by his interrogators. Mendoza disposes of the North Korean's Communist party card and admonishes him not to reveal his true status.

Chapters 5 and 6 are set at the American Army headquarters and deal with the torture and eventual murder of Kim. Determined to resist until death, Kim endures successive beatings to the point of unconsciousness. Mendoza is finally asked to take part in the interrogation as an interpreter. An American female army doctor named Jessica observes while Kim and Mendoza converse. Unbeknownst to Jack, Jessica understands Spanish and discovers that he is lying about Kim's testimony. Threatening Mendoza with a gun, she forces the Chicano to participate in the castration of the prisoner. She then approaches Mendoza sexually. He agrees to submit to her advances on the condition that she kill Kim to save him from further misery. Jessica accepts the proposition and the novel ends.

An interesting aspect of Motives is Revueltas's use of space and time to create a variety of fictional settings. Spatial delimitation, for instance, so favored in his novels, is strikingly present. The street scenes in Tijuana, reminiscent of those in In Some Valley of Tears, serve to reinforce the confusion and alienation experienced by the protagonist after his desertion. Mendoza is asphyxiated by the prisonlike atmosphere created by crowds and buildings. The Mascorros' garage and the interrogation room in Korea imprison the characters within four walls. In sharp contrast to the spatially delimited settings is the Korean wheat field, whose lyrical description recalls passages in The Stone Knife.

The time line in Motives begins on a given day during the early 1950s and proceeds in reverse chronological order, first to a period two weeks earlier and then to a point preceding both previous episodes. The Korean War as an historical setting is fictively merged with the Pachuco Wars in Los Angeles (1942-1943), the product of the Second World War.

The psychological ambience in Motives is one of violence, paranoia, alienation, and despair. It is, as

Floyd Merrell has observed, an "existential prison."[52]   With the brief exception of the Mascorros' house, where Mendoza finds a refuge, all other settings are negative to spirit and life. Salvador Reyes Nevares has stated: "In every corner of this book there runs a foul atmosphere of injustice and physical filth."[53]   Mendoza operates as the passive eye of history that records man's inhumanity concretely in racism and imperialism. His steadily worsening situation, beginning with the Korean incident, reduces him to a cowering, pathetic creature without a country.   Unable to cope with his complicity in war, he is rendered helpless and forced into flight.   But Mendoza's desertion in no way offers him an escape or salvation.   To the contrary, he is condemned to the role of an earthly vagabond who has lost his center of gravity.   Revueltas likens him to the Wandering Jew.   Ironically, although Mendoza is of Mexican ancestry, his sense of alienation in Tijuana is as great or greater than in the United States. Perhaps the novel's greatest strength resides in the characterization of Jack Mendoza as the central protagonist.   While the novel's other characters are little more than weak caricatures or stereotypes, Mendoza is one of Revueltas's memorable and complex fictional personages.   Distinctly apolitical, the Chicano lacks all historical consciousness and perspective.   While he is portrayed as ethical, his sense of right and wrong is blurred by his war experiences.   His participation in Kim's death has pushed him beyond the limits and he is now "on the other side of men."[54]   As Turón has indicated, Mendoza is "destroyed by the fanaticism and stupidity of other men; by the Korean War and by his human weaknesses, subject to fear, the sexual imperative, and inertia."[55]   As a rootless creature who is alienated from all societies and ports of refuge, Mendoza becomes a modern Cain who is shunned while he wanders as a fugitive.

Kim is clearly constructed as the positive hero in accord with orthodox Socialist Realism of the period. The North Korean is strong-willed, intelligent, and totally committed. He is the force of good that is vanquished by the evil forces of American Imperialism. His strength and courage permit him to endure to his death all attempts to make him submit to the interrogation and, thus, he triumphs over his captors. Kim's role is instructive, particularly for Mendoza, who until that moment has not seriously challenged his country's participation in the Korean War. Kim is, after Natividad in The Stone Knife, Revueltas's most exorbitant Communist hero. Essentially an unconvincing character, the North Korean's status as hero is achieved through relief with the other characters. Turón insists that Kim "is nothing more than a fanatic; but, the monsters that surround him, that reside within the limits of indecency, make him into the only man, the hero."56

Counterbalancing the positive symbols of Kim and the Mascorros is the American military. Jessica, the half-crazed, brutal, and perverse army doctor is characterized as a symbol of America's inhumanity. She calculatingly tortures Kim with a view to maximizing the pain. Tom, an infantryman in Mendoza's command, assumes ironic significance as a sensitive, Bible-reading, God-fearing American who actually relishes the violence of war. He is demonically a Christian warrior whose ethics and morality are heavily tinged with racism and hatred.

One character, Lutero Smith, deserves special mention. Although his presence is brief, it is

significant. When the deranged minister discovers
Mendoza hiding in the Mascorros' garage, he begins
to utter a mixture of prophetic, apocalyptic, and
condemnatory jabbering. Perhaps intended to
suggest a parallel with the biblical confrontation
between God and Cain, Smith accuses Mendoza of
having murdered a young boy in the barrio.
Mendoza's mental association is that of Kim,
however. This gratuitous association elevates the
crazy minister to an omniscient plane whereby he
extrapolates truth from his own mental disarray.

Stylistically, Motives is extremely uneven.
While at times the style is awkward and
tendentious, there are moments of great lyricism
and crafted narration. All in all, it is obvious that
Revueltas was not preoccupied with the novel's
literary quality, since the work's primary feature is
its unabated political propaganda, which
subordinates all artistic concerns. Nevertheless,
there are some noteworthy elements of style and
technique in the work. The reverse time sequence
employed is especially efficacious. Various
interesting effects are achieved through the use of
the Cain myth.[57] The characterization of
Mendoza, the street scenes in Tijuana, and the
controlled point of view are of merit. On the
other hand, the improbable plot (the appearance of
a North Korean from Culiacán), the awkward
mixture of Spanish and Kim's Korean-laminated
Spanish, and the outrageous stereotypes (Jessica and
Tom) are unconvincing.

Motives was a demonstration of Party faith for
Revueltas. As if to avoid all possible Party
criticism, he chose settings in two foreign
countries; his two protagonists are distinctly not
Mexican. The only references to the Party are in
the most general sense. No Party officials appear

and, therefore, no direct associations with Party leadership were possible such as was the case with Earthly Days. If Party critics were to find fault with the novel, it would have to be with its philosophical content. But Revueltas seemed to defuse any such possibility by adopting an aggressive anti-United States position, which incorporated an exposé of North American racism, coupled with a condemnation of the United States effort in Korea. In its largest sense, then, Motives is a highly politicized work that portrays the struggle between capitalism and international communism.

Politics is viewed not only globally but individually through the somewhat detached thoughts of Mendoza, who operates as a confused and uninformed evaluator of a chaotic world. Although the Chicano identifies in various ways with Kim and the Mascorros, on the other hand he is a product of the American military and American society. Unable to commit himself to one side or the other, he flees as a fugitive. Both politically and socially he suffers from an overwhelming alienation which, unfortunately, is not convincingly advanced by the author.

Numerous subthemes in Motives serve to support the fundamental question of political reality. Sex, death, violence and solitude inform the basic existential issues of choice and situation which confront Mendoza. As a modern existential Cain, Mendoza succumbs to aimlessness and exhaustion that nullify any hope of a politically redeeming or instructive stance. Nevertheless, the novel's intent is ambiguous; its message may reside equally in the heroics of Kim, or in the irresolution of Mendoza. The reader is presented with two classical models of contemporary literary types: the positive hero of

Socialist Realism and the existential antihero. The somewhat belabored blend of Marxism and existentialism, viewed respectively through the two protagonists, results in a lack of structure and unity; therefore, the novel fails to inform a coherent world view. But Revueltas's attempt to forge a satisfactory "whole" from two seemingly disparate philosophies deserves mention.

Revueltas was engaged in the same mission as that of Sartre and a host of leftist existentialist thinkers, namely, to forge an existentialist Marxism. The supposed existentialism of his earlier novels surfaces concretely in Motives in the form of Mendoza-Cain. Ruffinelli has observed: "Jack assumes on his shoulders the function of suffering a horrible world and intuiting that there is no escape. He is transformed into a man 'who flees' knowing that there is no way out."58 This very obvious existentialist posturing by Revueltas was acceptable in the mid-1950s as a result of Sartre's having embraced the Communist cause and the subsequent tolerance of an existential Marxism.59

Motives occupies a curious but important position in Revueltas's novelistic production. While it may be viewed as an inferior work, given to stereotyping, propagandizing and presenting improbable situations, it is not without literary value. More importantly, however, it reflects the attitudes, thoughts, and artistic concerns of Revueltas during a particularly crucial period of his life. Critical comment concerning the work has been sparse. Most critics view Motives as a marginal work. José Agustín, for example, considers it to be "Revueltas's weakest book, the most conventionally Marxist, whose only merit is its intent."60 Merrell views it as "thematically the weakest of Revueltas's novels."61 On the other hand, various reviewers have found value in the work. Mateo Sáenz viewed it as a novel that "contributes greatly to world peace since it unmasks the war makers who pretend to be 'defenders of democracy.'"[62]

Of all the existing evaluations concerning Motives, the most creative has come from Evodio Escalante, who views both The Motives of Cain, and In Some Valley of Tears as representative of a "kind of self-induced 'purge,' a demonstration of sterility, the unproductive attempt to write literature observing the norms of an insipid and prefabricated realism."[63] Whether or not Escalante's thesis was consciously at work in the 1950s with Revueltas is speculative. In retrospect, however, such a notion takes on considerable significance, particularly when considering the author's sixth novel, Errors.

Errors (1964)

Revueltas's last expulsion from the Mexican Communist party in 1960 anticipated his most ambitious and complex novel. Los errores (Errors) was to be the author's final and definitive novelistic treatment of politics and the Party. In large part, the work was an elaboration of the political and ethical positions developed in Earthly Days some fifteen years earlier. Errors, however, was cast in a much larger historical and philosophical framework than its predecessor. Instead of attacking the Mexican Communist party, Revueltas sought to discredit the entire international Communist movement, targeting specifically on the Soviet regime of Stalin in the 1930s.

In spite of its blanket denunciation of Soviet and Mexican Communism, <u>Errors</u> did not provoke the scathing attacks that <u>Earthly Days</u> had incited. While Marxist critics viewed the novel with general disfavor, few attempted to refute Revueltas's analysis of Stalinism, since Marxists themselves now openly admitted excesses and "errors" of Stalin and the cult of personality. Nevertheless, the publication of <u>Errors</u> placed Jose Revueltas in the enemy camp <u>from</u> the Communist officialdom's point of view.

<u>Errors</u> consists of twenty-seven chapters and an epilogue. Two separate plot lines, initially having nothing to do with each other, develop simultaneously. Eventually the two plots interweave, finally merging into a unified whole at the end of the novel. The implementation of two parallel plots invites the reader to observe Revueltas's view of dialectics in action, but the task is not easy. <u>Errors</u> requires careful and reconstructive <u>reading</u> that forces one to differentiate independent and unrelated actions with those that are causally related.

The first plot deals with a robbery perpetrated by a young pimp, Mario Cobián, and his accomplice, a homosexual dwarf named Elena. The two unsavory characters plan to rob Don Victorino, a wealthy moneylender. The plan is simple; Cobián will carry Elena in a suitcase and deposit him in Victorino's shop. Later, after Victorino has left for the day, Elena will emerge, unlock the door from within, and admit Cobián. The plan misfires, though, when Elena appears from the suitcase prematurely, only to find Victorino still present in the shop. Gripped with fear, Elena viciously slays the moneylender with a knife. In the meantime, Cobián has been searching for his prostitute girl friend, Luque, with whom he plans to run away and start a new life in the North of Mexico. It is to be the spoils of the robbery that will provide them with the means to escape from their sordid existence in the Mexico City underworld. Unable to find Luque either at her apartment or at the tavern where she works, Cobián encounters another prostitute, La Magnífica, who informs him that Luque is going to run away with another man. In a rage, Cobián returns to Luque's apartment, where he now finds her and brutally beats her. Leaving her for dead, he then proceeds to Victorino's and discovers the plan has gone awry. Cobián collects the money, orders Elena into the suitcase, and starts walking through the streets. Crossing a sewage canal, he suddenly decides to rid himself of the repulsive and troublesome dwarf by shoving the suitcase off the bridge. Shortly thereafter, Cobián is arrested by the police for his assault on Luque. In a panic he confesses to the robbery of Victorino, as well as to the murder of Elena. In addition, he eagerly supplies details concerning Elena's murder of the moneylender.

The second plot line deals with the preparation and execution of an armed assault on the headquarters of the Mexican Anticommunist Union by a group of Communist militants. The assault is planned as a cover for the assassination of Eladio Pintos, who has been accused by the Party of a variety of sectarian crimes, including plotting to assassinate Stalin and supporting Trotskyism. Demonically, the party has commissioned Pintos to organize the very assault that is to lead to his own death. Unfortunately for the Party, Pintos discovers that he is to be murdered during the assault and enlists the aid of his old comrade Olegario Chávez, whom he had known in the Soviet

Union. Chávez promises to thwart the Party's
secret assassin, a linotypist, when the latter
attempts to carry out the orders against Pintos.
The attack against the Fascist headquarters
involves a number of Party workers, including
Januario López, a taxi driver; Samuel Morfín, a
storekeeper; Eusebio Cano, a streetcar operator;
and Niágara, a young Party worker. Although the
assault is planned with precision, it fails because
the Fascists, having been forewarned, evacuate
their offices. When the actual assault occurs, only
one Fascist leader, Nazario Villegas, is present. In
the midst of much confusion, Villegas succeeds in
killing Morfín and fleeing. Chávez disarms the
linotypist and then kills Niágara, a Trotskyite whom
Chávez had been ordered to assassinate. Pintos,
López and Cano escape. The police promptly
arrive and arrest Chávez for murder.

The two plot lines definitively merge when
Chávez and Cobián are both detained at police
headquarters. Chávez, who was Victorino's
bookkeeper, is charged with the latter's death, even
though the police know through Cobián's confession
that Elena was the perpetrator. Cobián, in
exchange for his silence, is offered a job as a
police agent; Cobián's murder of Elena will be
conveniently forgotten.

The novel ends with an epilogue titled El nudo
ciego (The Blind Knot). It primarily treats a long
and complicated discussion between Patricio Robles,
the local head of the Mexican Communist party,
and Ismael Cabrera, another Party official. The
two men vigorously debate the decisions to expel
Olegario and Eladio Pintos from the Party. In the
process, Revueltas recapitulates his message on

Party obligation and individual freedom and responsibility. The epilogue ends with a brief encounter between Cobián and Luque in the hospital.

In addition to the two primary plot lines, a major subplot emerges which deals with the case of Jacobo Ponce, a university professor and Party intellectual. Ponce is consumed with researching the history of Emilio Padilla, a Mexican Communist who had disappeared in the Soviet Union. As a result of his research, Ponce has determined that Padilla has been unjustly imprisoned in the Soviet Union and is being held incommunicado. Since Ponce's study, if released, threatens to embarrass the Communist party in Mexico, he is ordered by Ismael Cabrera to cease his work immediately or suffer expulsion from the Party for his ideological distortions. In the process of his study, Ponce develops a concept of the Party as an "ethical notion," an idea for which he is soundly criticized.[64] Revueltas devotes significant segments of his narrative to reflect the internal emotional and intellectual struggles that face Ponce regarding his relationship with the Party.

The two primary plot lines yield a multitude of secondary episodes and anecdotes which are related in flashback. Some of the more noteworthy are: Mario Cobián's childhood and his relationship with his mother; Cobián's association with a young female entertainer, Jovita Layton; Victorino's experiences in the Mexican Revolution; Luque's childhood; her subsequent marriage to Ralph and their life in New York City; Olegario's escape from a Mexico City prison through a sewer system; the trial of Olenka Delnova in Moscow; and various exploits of Eladio Pintos.

The action in the primary plot lines occurs in a two-day period in 1940. Through numerous episodic flashbacks, Revueltas sweeps back in time to collect incidents throughout the entire decade of the 1930s. Certainly his most documental novel, Errors is based on historical events in Mexico and the Soviet Union. In the case of the former, Revueltas re-creates the bitter conflict between fascism and communism waged in the streets of Mexico City. In all probability, the historical prototype for Revueltas's fictional Fascist organization, the Unión Mexicana Anticomunista, is, as Marco Antonio Millán suggests, the infamous "los dorados. . . ."[65] In any event, the intrigue, hatred, and rivalry between the Communists and Fascists in Mexico City during the 1930s were an intimate part of José Reveultas's formative years. No less pertinent to Revueltas's biography are the numerous segments dealing with the Soviet Union under Stalin, particularly the Moscow Trials of 1936, which were in preparation during Revueltas's first visit to that country. In all, Errors, like its predecessor, Earthly Days, intimately reflects concrete historical-political events of the decade.

The setting for both primary plots is Mexico City--its streets and buildings. Thus, Errors is clearly Revueltas's most urban novel. As the narrative moves from one specific locale to another within Mexico City, the reader falls victim to Revueltas's fondness for creating hermetic, asphyxiating spatial cubicles. Cobián's hotel room, Victorino's store, and Magdalena's apartment are but a few examples. Two instances of extreme spatial delimitation occur: Elena's confinement in the suitcase and Olegario's prison escape through the rat-infested sewer lines. These intense hermetic enclosures are effectively contrasted with scenes in the Soviet Union, achieved through flashbacks to attain an international perspective.

The psychological ambience in <u>Errors</u> is one of fear, violence, intrigue, paranoia, and corruption. The majority of the action occurs in unsavory locales. Many of the characters' personalities and actions reflect their sordid existence. Perversion, crime, and violent acts are common to all. Mirroring Revueltas's fundamentally pessimistic view of mankind, <u>Errors</u> may be seen as a huge receptacle containing most of the common types developed in the previous novels. The despair and distrust attendant to the robbery plot are suspiciously those qualities ever present in the political plot. These two parallel stories are structurally merged precisely as a result of the proximity of the two worlds in which each respective story unfolds.

The merging is achieved through a series of coincidences (some are a bit unlikely) and fortuitous events that bring the two autonomous trajectories to a single conclusion. For example, the Communist Olegario Chávez coincidentally is a bookkeeper for Victorino, a Fascist supporter and friend of Nazario Villegas. Thus, when Cobián and Elena carry out their crime against the moneylender, they are posed for an encounter with the political sphere. Mario, in searching for Luque, hails the taxicab of Januario López, a participant in the assault on the Fascists' headquarters. Olegario and Eusebio Cano meet to discuss Party matters in the restaurant of La Jaiba, one of Cobián's mistresses. While there, they observe Cobián, who mistakenly assumes that they are police agents. Shortly after the robbery, while walking through the streets, Cobián once again accidentally encounters Olegario, further reinforcing his notion that Olegario is a police agent who is pursuing him. Another fortuitous connection between the two plots occurs as a result of Villegas's activities. He appears in the robbery plot by visiting the moneylender's shop on two occasions. He also appears in the political plot as the only Fascist present during the assault on their headquarters. The various narrative coincidences coalesce to a climax when Cobián, through police coercion, agrees to remain silent concerning Elena's murder of Victorino so that the authorities may prosecute Olegario as the assassin. The end result is that the sometimes strained coincidences serve as structural ligatures that slowly and methodically draw the two apparently disparate plots together to achieve a final solution.

One of the most notable features of Errors is its wide array of characters; in many ways the novel is a collection of personalities. With few exceptions, the characters belong either to the robbery plot or to the political plot. The former is populated primarily by members of Mexico City's underworld. The plot is actualized, first and foremost, through the thoughts and actions of Mario Cobián, perhaps the best developed of the characters. Viewed as a confused, victimized product of a corrupt society, Cobián decides to change his life-style definitively for the better. He is, as Revueltas once said, "an ethical being who adopts ethical decisions."[66] He is motivated by love and his distaste for his involvement in prostitution. Unfortunately, his only means to disengage himself and Luque from their desperate existence is to commit a criminal act. Three prostitutes, La Jaiba, La Magnífica, and Luque (Lucrecia), are presented. Only Luque assumes prominence in the narrative, however, as Cobián's object of affection. Interestingly enough, when once asked to cite his favorite character in his novels, Revueltas replied: "I like Lucrecia a lot, in Errors, because she represents very well her existential condition."[67]   Luque's formative years are presented via flashback. Scarred by life's misfortunes and unable to escape from her circumstances, Luque pathetically tells Cobián: "You can do with me what you want. Hit me, mistreat me, humiliate me. I know that I cannot escape you."[68]   She concludes that only death will free her.

The most unusual personage in Errors is clearly Elena, the homosexual dwarf, a "primitive character of irrational passions."[69]   Operating as Cobián's accomplice in the robbery, Elena is utterly perverse and, with the possible exception of El Carajo in The Isolation Cell, the most grotesque and vulgar creature to be found anywhere in Revueltas's novels.   As such, he functions as the ultimate symbol of the deformed and debased lower strata of Mexican society, the very place from which Cobián wishes to escape.

In the political plot, Revueltas offers a full spectrum of Communist militants ranging from dogmatic Stalinists to free-thinking revisionists. The very central theme of orthodoxy versus unorthodoxy takes on form and meaning primarily through the thoughts and actions of these men. Noteworthy is the manner in which Revueltas has totally inverted the role of the traditional positive hero, so that the Party faithful is viewed as overly dogmatic and unable to attain superior moral stature.[70]   Conversely, the Party heretics are elevated to true hero status precisely because they are in opposition to the Party and Stalinism.   This approach to the hero, initiated in Earthly Days, is developed without restraint in Errors. Importantly, many if not all of the Party militants are disguised versions of actual Mexican Communists who were active in the 1930s. By changing their names slightly, Revueltas, in effect, put them on public trial in his novel.

Jacobo Ponce, like Gregorio in Earthly Days, is clearly the author's intellectual persona with respect to Stalinism and revisionism. Turón observes: "Jacobo Ponce's reflections prolong and extend the thought of Gregorio Saldívar, the hero of Earthly Days."71 While Ponce is not a man of action, he is a man of courage. When faced with expulsion he stays his ground, ethically determined to ferret out the truth about Padilla.

Emilio Padilla is a good example of Revueltas's altering of real names of real people. The character is patterned after Evelio Vadillo, a "law student in Mexico who was given a scholarship to study in the Soviet Union and who, upon returning, encountered a mysterious death."72 Padilla, like Ponce, was expelled from the Party for speaking openly in cell groups. Clearly a victim of the Stalinist purges, he achieves a certain vague status of martyr in Errors. He does not, however, assume an active role in the narrative, but rather is only presented through flashbacks.

Olegario Chávez, a rank-and-file Party militant, complements Ponce to present fully the author's persona. He is essentially a man of action, albeit capable of self-analysis. His natural evolution as a character results in his expulsion. Thoroughly a man of principle, he is overcome with guilt upon assassinating Niágara by dictate of the Party. If Ponce is an extension of Gregorio Saldívar's intellectualism, Chávez is an extension of Gregorio with respect to action. Thus, Ponce and Olegario, the intellectual and the man of action, seen jointly, are clearly José Revueltas--theoretician and activist. They are morally superior men whose political heresy and subsequent expulsion underline their status as Communist heroes.

Eladio Pintos, curiously, is a fusion of Chávez and Ponce. As a kind of international Communist celebrity presented with a tinge of romanticism, Pintos has been branded a Party heretic. Somewhat reminiscent of Natividad in The Stone Knife, he is characterized as strong, intelligent, and capable. In short, he is an heroic leader who inspires his comrades, particularly Olegario, to action. When once asked to comment on Pintos, Ponce, and Chávez, Revueltas pointed to both their historical significance and their autobiographical nature: "They are what we would call historical personages who underline a personal direction, a coincidence with the author because they are the author himself in various invented and re-created situations."[73]

In sharp contrast to the four expelled Party members, who function as true heroes, are Patricio Robles and Ismael Cabrera. While neither character assumes a major role in the novel, their presence is critical to the execution of the primary thesis under study in Errors. Both Robles and Cabrera represent extreme orthodoxy, blind dogmatism, lack of self-analysis, and paralysis of will. Even though Cabrera, at one point, appears to question the wisdom of Party decisions, he quickly retreats and sides with the dictatorial Robles. Presented as caricatures, they are puppetlike in their defense of and deference to Party dictates and Stalinism.

Other Party workers appear, including Eusebio Cano, an unenlightened but dedicated Communist

who blindly obeys orders; Januario López, whose
Party loyalty is so extreme that he kills his wife
for fear that she will inform the police of his
activities; and the linotypist, whose unquestioning
adherence to Party orders enables him to agree to
assassinate Eladio Pintos. These men, while
examples of dogmatic righteousness, are not
vigorously condemned by Revueltas because they do
not possess the necessary intellectual capacity to
fathom their "errors." In addition, there is
Niágara, a somewhat enigmatic Trotskyite, and
Samuel Morfín, a successful store owner and Party
sympathizer.

The Mexican bourgeois power structure is
represented by five characters, each in a particular
way. Vittorio Amino, a sort of international
playboy whose nationality is never mentioned, is
associated with Magdalena, a presumably well-to-do
woman who has an affair with Amino and Ponce
simultaneously. It is Amino who finally provides
Ponce with definitive proof of Padilla's
imprisonment in the Soviet Union. Perhaps the
best symbol of the bourgeoisie is Victorino, who
figures prominently but passively in both plots.
Portrayed as an odious moneylender and blatant
racist, he is an active supporter of the Fascists'
cause in Mexico. In the robbery plot, he is the
object of Cobián's aggression; in the political plot,
his death coalesces the action and results in the
false accusation of Olegario. Finally, the
bourgeoisie is reflected in the thoughts and actions
of Nazario Villegas, the cunning and cruel Fascist
leader, and by Commander Villalobos, the conniving
and very political police chief. If there are
winners in the novel, they are Villegas and
Villalobos, for they receive the immediate benefit
of a long series of errors.

Stylistically, <u>Errors</u> incorporates most of the literary devices utilized in Revueltas's other novels. Such items as flashbacks, cinematographic play with time and space, interior monologues, reliance on rough vernacular, hermetic enclosures to potentiate tension, biting realism, and intercalated anecdotes that amount to short stories, are all present. Perhaps more than any other novel, <u>Errors</u> was soundly criticized for its defects in style and narrative technique. Nevertheless, there are episodes in the work that present Revueltas as a master narrator. One such instance is Olegario's escape through the sewer system. Another is the description of Elena inside Cobián's suitcase. These episodes, as well as others, counterbalance the rather tedious and clumsily inserted polemics that supposedly reflect the characters' thinking.

The themes and issues under discussion in <u>Errors</u> are numerous and diverse, so much so that this study can do little more than point to the more obvious and salient topics. The novel quickly immerses the reader in a myriad of philosophical, ethical, political, and social questions which interconnect in a dizzying web of speculations and assertions. In varying degrees of relief are such topics as man and society, man and the state, historical materialism, the ethics of Marxism, communism versus fascism, Party orthodoxy versus unorthodoxy, Stalinism, social and economic determinism, alienation, individual responsibility, human freedom, existentialism versus the absolutes of Marxism, and the constituents of the positive hero. These issues, as well as many others, easily make <u>Errors</u> Revueltas's most profound and intricate novel. It is, in fact, a compendium of Revueltas's views as a political theoretician, thinker, and artist, developed over some thirty years.

First and foremost, <u>Errors</u> is a political novel in which politics itself becomes the primary subject. Revueltas tackles the political confrontation between Communists and Fascists at the anecdotal level for the purpose of developing and extrapolating several other major political concerns. In examining the local "errors" of the Mexican Communists, the larger issue of Stalinism as an organizing principle for international communism emerges. By logical extension, the question of Party orthodoxy, both at the local and international level, is analyzed. This topic, in turn, evolves into a consideration of Party ethics and individual responsibility in the face of unrestrained dogmatism. These global issues are concretized in the persons of Ponce and Chávez as they ponder their relationship to the Party.

The umbrella issues of historical materialism and economic determinism are ever present. Cobián's criminal act is predicated on an economic imperative. In a similar fashion, Victorino's entire life is an economic venture to the point that it is the basis of his very existence. At the same time, Ponce and Chávez, like all faithful Communists, are committed to a definitive redistribution of wealth. Revueltas goes to great length to illustrate the movement of reality in dialectical fashion based on a Marxist notion of materialism and economic determinism, whereby all the characters, whether implicitly or explicitly, are trapped within fixed social and economic limits.

Not all the questions and issues posed by Revueltas in <u>Errors</u> are clearly answered, but several are definitively resolved. The author, for instance, specifically denounces Stalinism and the Party's tactics during the 1930s. He further condemns bourgeois culture and the Fascist movement. He creates a new model of the positive hero whereby the Party member who seeks such status must break with the Party. He carries the idea of man as an "inexact creature," posited by Gregorio in Earthly Days, to a further limit whereby Ponce concludes that man is an "erroneous being." In addition, he allows Ponce to postulate the concept of the Party as an ethical notion. Revueltas successfully defends the concept of man as a creature determined within certain spatial, temporal, and historical conditions from which he cannot escape. Most importantly, the novel affirms and confirms "errors" as a condition fundamental to man.

Critical reaction to Errors was mixed. Emmanuel Carballo criticized the heavy-handed presentation of thesis, the unconvincing characters, the intrusive presence of the author, and the chaotic structure.[74] Mauricio de la Selva, echoing a subdued Marxist complaint, accused Revueltas of excessive subjectivity in his attack on the Party.[75] Errors was not without its promoters, however. Carmen Andrade concluded that the work must be recognized for its "truth, elegance of prose, and shocking psychological penetration, elements that captivate."[76] One critic, somewhat hyperbolically, stated: "Errors is literally an accumulation of narrative achievements. An exceptional novel."[77] Sadot Fabila H. was no less complimentary: "Seen in its entirety, as a novelistic whole, Errors is a great work that affirms its universal stature with its quality of testimony of events which occurred in a moment in Mexican history."[78]

While the initial reviews and criticisms ranged from mild, politically motivated attacks to positive critical rhetoric, Errors has continued to gain support among students of Revueltas's novels through the ensuing years. For a majority of readers, it is his best novel, although the issue is much debated. What is certain is that Errors is Revueltas's most mature novel from both a political and philosophical standpoint. On the other hand, the many criticisms leveled at the work for defects in style, poor character development, reliance on contrived coincidence, overstatement of thesis, awkward composition, and repetitive lead-ins to monologues, are not without substance. Nonetheless, Errors must be considered Revueltas's single most important novel.

The Isolation Cell (1969)

Revueltas wrote his last novel during the months of February and March 1969, shortly after being sent to Lecumberri Prison.[79] Utilizing his very real and awesome experiences endured in the infamous Black Palace of Lecumberri, he elaborated a stunning fictional narration that was an immediate literary success. El apando (The Isolation Cell) consists of forty-six printed pages and, by both its extension and complexity, falls somewhere between the genres of short story and novelette. Since most critics, as well as Revueltas, have considered the work to be a novel, it is included in this study as such.

The action begins in an isolation cell where three prisoners have been confined, apparently as punishment for infractions unspecified in the narrative. The three men have one thing in common: all are involved in an attempt to smuggle drugs into the prison. Two of the inmates, Polonio and Albino, are friends and fellow drug traffickers within the prison. The third man, El Carajo, is a deformed and almost moronic addict who is openly despised by the other two men. This hapless trio hopes to obtain twenty to thirty grams of an unspecified drug with the help of three women: Polonio's girl friend, La Chata; Albino's girl friend, Meche and El Carajo's old mother.

The three prisoners and their female associates concoct a plan to smuggle drugs into the prison by concealing them in a feminine sanitary tampon. Since La Chata and Meche are routinely given gynecological searches when entering the prison for visits, they are eliminated as potential carriers of the contraband. El Carajo's mother, on the other hand, because of her age and general demeanor, is not subjected to such an inspection. Thus, the mother is recruited to be the surreptitious conveyer of the narcotics. Believing them to be destined for her addict son, she readily agrees to participate in the operation. La Chata and Meche are charged with helping her insert the tampon properly. Because prisoners in isolation are not permitted visitors, the three women must name other inmates as the object of their visit. Once inside the prison, they are to proceed inconspicuously to the isolation cell where they are to create a general disturbance, with the hope of having the men released from isolation.

The plan goes well initially, with the women passing undetected through the inspection. Upon arriving at the cell, however, their disturbance is quickly quelled by the guards and the three prisoners are ordered out of the isolation cell. Unable to effect the transfer of the drugs, the six men and women are marched to a security cage where, the prison Commandant promises, they will be able to conduct the visit. After entering the cage, though, the guards manage, through trickery, to force the three women outside the cage through another door. Reacting in a rage to the obvious deceit, Albino suddenly locks the Commandant and several guards inside the cage, along with himself and his two cellmates. Exploding in uncontrollable anger, Polonio and Albino physically assault the prison officers. The attack ends when a large group of guards arrives with long metal tubes which they quickly insert into the cell, methodically to reduce the area of battle, finally trapping the three prisoners and putting an end to the brief rebellion.

Both temporal and spatial elements in The Isolation Cell are sharply delimited. While the narrative provides no specific indication of actual elapsed time, the transpired action suggests a period in the neighborhood of an hour. Although the story is atemporal in an historical sense, it clearly corresponds to conditions prevalent in Lecumberri in 1969. The novel's spatial elements are those of the prison: an isolation cell, the corridor of a cellblock, a visitor's room, and a security cage. Spatial delimitation as a narrative device reaches maximum expression in Isolation Cell. The action is compartmentalized in various cubicles which are hermetically sealed from one another. To trace out a sense of separate spatial components Revueltas utilizes geometrical terminology and designs whereby both concrete reality and mankind's condition are projected in geometric patterns. The repeated use of angles, planes, triangles, trapezoids, parameters, and so forth makes space and geometry keys to unlocking meaning. Specifically, Revueltas himself commented on an "alienated geometry" in Isolation Cell in which man is not only alienated in a physical sense, but also with respect to thought and knowledge.[80]

Fear and violence dominate the mood and action in Isolation Cell. The effect on the characters is to degrade and ultimately dehumanize them. The sheer intensity of isolation exacerbates the prisoners' baser emotions. Both inmates and guards are reduced to a kind of subhuman existence. Their only purpose is to continue to occupy prescribed areas of the prison. A persistent sense of oppression and frustration pushes the prisoners to the threshold of irrationality. Thus, Polonio and Albino almost casually decide to kill El Carajo once the drugs are obtained, apparently for no other reason than a general disgust that El Carajo provokes in them. El Carajo routinely cuts his veins in order to escape from the cell block by being sent to the infirmary. In all, Revueltas forcefully creates a living hell from which no one escapes. Descriptive passages, actions, language, and personalities meld into a powerful narration that entraps the reader within what is presumably the world of Lecumberri Prison.

Although the brevity of Isolation Cell tends to restrict character development, Revueltas does, in fact, succeed in creating some memorable narrative types who are, almost unbelievably, based on actual people.[81] There are six primary characters who represent three distinct pairs: Polonio–La Chata, Albino–Meche, and El Carajo–Mother. Polonio and Albino control the narrative's point of view. Their close association as colleagues is based on their mutual activities and confinement. Both men are portrayed as tough, prison-wise inmates who have turned incarceration into profit through their drug dealings. As the author of the plan to smuggle drugs into the prison, Polonio assumes a certain stature as the more dominant member of the duo. But it is Albino who comes to the forefront in the narrative. His most noteworthy characteristic is a large tatoo on his stomach portraying a couple copulating. Albino enjoys considerable status in the prison for his ability to entertain and titillate the other prisoners. He is a sort of fulcrum of eroticism. At the novel's end it is Albino who acts decisively by locking the group in the security cage.

El Carajo, unlike his two cellmates, is a grotesque creature who is totally dependent on drugs. Given to self-mutilation, he is a physical monstrosity and is utterly worthless. Even his mother wishes that he would die. Although his role in the novel is entirely passive, El Carajo's mere existence drives his cellmates to the point of murder and his mother to commit a criminal act. His one coherent utterance in the narrative occurs when he pathetically, but importantly, informs the guards of his mother's participation in the smuggling operation. In short, he is a wretched protoplasmic specimen. In spite of the negative characterization, however, Revueltas has argued that El Carajo is an ethical being who stands out as the only self-conscious and self-critical character in the novel.[82]

The three female characters are viewed in relationship to their men. La Chata and Meche are the least developed, representing little more than sexual objects who willingly do the bidding of Polonio and Albino. Portrayed as loose women, they are, nevertheless, honorable and faithful companions to their men. The other female character, El Carajo's mother, is the most interesting. While she demonstrates honest motherly love in her concern for her son, she feeds

his dangerous addiction, all the time wishing that
he would die. Revueltas suggests a kind of bovine
creature who has been used throughout her life
and, indeed, is now being exploited by her son and
his cellmates. The mother is perhaps best
understood as a primitive maternal force that
instinctively seeks to protect and comfort her
offspring irrespective of all contrary conditions and
signs.

Rounding out the cast of characters are
numerous nameless prison guards whose very
anonymity underlines the author's notion that they
are, in fact, also prisoners who senselessly act out
their role, unaware of their own incarceration. In
using prison slang to refer to the guards as monos
("monkeys"), Revueltas portrays them as stupid,
lower primates who walk the parameters of their
respective cages (realities) in endless boredom. Of
the guards, only the Commandant is individualized,
and then only to permit him to deceive the
prisoners.

Stylistically, Isolation Cell rates as one of
Revueltas's very best narrative pieces. Written in
one long paragraph, the narration reflects the
hermetic nature of the prison world and the
isolation cell. The work is constructed with great
precision and care, and is devoid of the usual long,
cumbersome digressions that plague the other
novels. Language is of paramount importance in
the narration. Utilizing a richly adjectivized
syntax, along with symbols and metaphors,
Revueltas skillfully weaves a combination of prison
and street slang into standard language to produce
a powerful style totally congruent with the
material under treatment. The result is a small
narrative jewel where language becomes the
centerpiece. Manuel Blanco has observed: "The

clean language, totally depurated and of an incredible audacity, is perfectly suited to the story and its development, and suddenly, perhaps without the author's intending, it becomes the substratum of the entire work."[83]

One of the novel's most impressive components is its manipulation of point of view. Employing a cinematographic narrator's eye, Revueltas exaggerates the effect in Isolation Cell, where much of the action is viewed by either Polonio or Albino as they take turns gazing through a small opening in the cell door. Effectively destroying all peripheral view of reality, the author obstructs the reader's ability to survey the setting panoramically. Thus, as Argelio Gasca has observed, Revueltas "sees his characters and they in turn see others: always through the keyhole with a perennial incomplete vision, capturing creatures instantaneously, only from one of the latters' precarious angles."[84] As a technical device, the reduced narrative aperture effectively intensifies the sense of incarceration, while it simultaneously underscores the novel's great metaphoric value as a statement of man's philosophic isolation and alienation.

Numerous other narrative patterns and devices are employed in Isolation Cell. Revueltas relies on such items as biblical myth, zoological characterization, suggestive imagery bordering on erotica, cinematographic time play, and the purposeful exclusion of auditory elements. In all, these and other stylistic elements are part of a large, judiciously executed narrative that is a significant testament to Revueltas's skill as a master narrator.

In addition to the stunning stylistic achievements found in Isolation Cell, the work is noteworthy for its philosophic content and its treatment of various recurrent Revueltian themes. As Juan Tovar has concluded, the novel is the "quintessential example of Revueltian thought."[85] Tovar's very correct assessment is surprising when one considers that Isolation Cell is completely nonpolitical at the surface level, a phenomenon witnessed only previously in the case of In Some Valley of Tears. Particularly curious and perhaps ironic is the fact that Revueltas's imprisonment in Lecumberri was a major political event. That Revueltas refused to dissect politically his incarceration, as well as that of his fellow revolutionaries, speaks directly to his maturity as a thinker and writer. Clearly, Revueltas had abandoned his preoccupation with the Party and thesis-ladened Communist pronouncements as his primary novelistic themes. Isolation Cell, on the contrary, reflects a decided effort to elevate his last prison experience to an abstract and philosophical level without reference to practical politics.

If the anecdote is depoliticized, the extrapolated speculations in the novel still faithfully underscore the author's continued meditations on man and society, in both political and philosophical terms. As Revueltas once pointed out, the isolation cell and prison are but metaphors for society, where men are prisoners of history, of culture and finally of themselves. Exercising a sharp critical realism, Revueltas makes a definitive statement concerning alienation, a cardinal tenet in his highly evolved and highly personal interpretation of Marxism. Noticeably, this particular rendition is existentialist in its orientation. Thus the daringly revisionist evaluation of Marxism which was begun in Earthly

Days culminates as a central thesis in Isolation Cell.

Revueltas began and ended his production of novels with treatments of incarceration based on actual imprisonments suffered throughout his life. While both Walls of Water and Isolation Cell share thematic similarities, it is the latter that succeeds in fully explicating Revueltas's theory of knowledge, his conceptualization of dialectical thought and movement (particularly its potential for negative flow), and his evaluation of society and its relationship to man. When the two novels in question are compared and contrasted, there emerges not only a disparity of sophistication but also a determined shift from Marxian idealism to existential realism. This drift, long in evidence throughout the trajectory of Revueltas's novels, concretely reveals itself in a comparison between his first and last novels.

Critical reaction to Isolation Cell has been uniformly favorable; for many, the work is considered to be the best single example of Revueltian narrative. The novel's popularity was further underscored in 1975 when José Agustín, with the close counsel of Revueltas, converted the novel to a screenplay. For many years literary critics had waited anxiously for Revueltas to produce his great Mexican novel. Whether or not he fulfilled their expectations with Isolation Cell is questionable, but it remains the only probable candidate for such an honorable status because it is precisely this work that exhibits Revueltas at his best as both a thinker and a writer.

Chapter Three

The Short Stories

José Revueltas was a superb and prolific short-story writer. His reputation as such was established early in his literary career and continues. Unlike his rather uneven reception as a novelist, his stature as a storyteller places him comfortably among the best in Latin America. Revueltas's contribution to the genre was of such importance that, in all likelihood, it may be considered his greatest literary achievement. Particularly within Mexican literature it is difficult to overstate Revueltas's influence upon the short-story writers associated with the so-called "new narrative." Indeed, as Luis Leal has suggested: "The new short story in Mexico cannot be satisfactorily explained without considering his contribution to its development."[1] But Revueltas's role was not only that of innovator; his own works disclose a literary genius that generated a short fiction that is the object of admiration for discerning critics. José Agustín has echoed the general critical consensus: "In Mexico only Juan Rulfo and Juan José Arreola have ever written short stories as great as those of Revueltas."[2] Díez de Urdanivia has argued Revueltas's greatness on a more continental scale: "It has been said that Revueltas forms, with Julio Cortázar, the best pair of Latin American short-story writers."[3] María Josefina Tejera underlines Revueltas's importance by stating that his stories "can be compared with the best in the Spanish language."[4]

Like most Latin American writers, Revueltas found it relatively easy to publish his short fiction in literary journals. His first novel, however, could be published only through the use of private funds from family and friends. Thus, his initial inclination toward the short story was, in part, economic. Unlike many novelists, though, who tend to abandon short fiction once attaining stature as a novelist, Revueltas continued to ply his craft as a storyteller throughout his literary career. Indeed, he forever displayed a predilection for the genre. Even in his novels many of the most memorable episodes are nothing but intercalated stories. Revueltas's natural proclivity to the short story prompted María del Carmen Millán to assert that the short story was the genre "best suited to the creative capacity of Revueltas."[5]

Revueltas's role as an initiator of the modern Mexican short story parallels in many ways his role as innovator in the novel. In general terms, Revueltas synthesized the two major literary currents of his day: the externalized, realistic narrative, best represented by the short story of the Mexican Revolution; and the poetic, symbolic, and psychological trend of "imaginative literature." Nevertheless, the parallel, which has been simplified for commentary purposes, must not be taken too far. As Luis Leal has aptly observed: "The short story has its own trajectory, it has developed in a completely different manner from that of the novel."[6] Perhaps the primary reason centers on the question of mode of production. For purely economic reasons, the successful publication of a novel was a considerable financial project. Thus the acceptance or rejection of a novel was often based on marketing principles that could greatly affect the novel's content and style. On the other hand, the short story typically found its way into print through newspapers and magazines. This fact was significant for two reasons. In the first place, there being little or no financial commitment, short stories were readily accepted for publication in Latin America. In the second place, unlike the novel, the short story was directed to a much larger readership. This consideration, in turn, often controlled the author's point of view, style, and theme. Finally, the very nature of the short story, its brevity and singular impact, differed considerably from the more extended narrative found in the novel.

In any event, Leal's point, which is often overlooked or underemphasized with regard to the origin and evolution of Latin American narrative, is essential. It is clear that the short story and the novel responded to different literary impulses and organizing principles and thus developed along different lines. This bifurcation is particularly pronounced in Revueltas's fiction, in which there are unique substantive differences between his novels and his short stories.

From Realism and its subscribers, Revueltas inherited his characters, settings, and situations. From the imaginative current, Revueltas cultivated a poetical, symbolic, and connotative language and style that sought to probe the psychological interior of his characters, clearly at the expense of a superficial, action-oriented plot. In doing so, Revueltas placed himself in the mainstream of contemporary North American and European short fiction. Although he would later cultivate a more traditional narrative mode, his early practice of reducing the importance of plot, virtually eliminating dialogue and fragmenting the chronological time line, was an attempt to give new artistic credibility to the short story. He relied heavily on omniscient narration and the creation of unique, sometimes rarefied atmospheres. Revueltas often placed his characters in extreme, stressful situations, bordering on the violent, the perverse, and the bizarre. Even though Revueltas's short stories are often locked within the unique world of Mexican culture, he sought to imbue them with universal meaning. He achieved this by relentlessly probing the psyche of his characters at its most basic level and thus exposing man in his most fundamental and existential state.

Considerable emphasis must be assigned to the essential differences between Revueltas's novels and his short stories. While the former are highly politicized, the latter, with few exceptions, are devoid of politics. Whereas the novels are often fraught with awkwardness and turgidity of style, the short stories are noteworthy for their literary craftsmanship. Not surprisingly, Revueltas's best novel from a stylistic point of view, The Isolation Cell, is considered by some critics to be an extended short story. Thus, one can envision a dialectical opposition between Revueltas's efforts in the two genres. While political philosophy and practical politics clearly prevail in the novels at the expense of literariness, the majority of the short stories neither promote nor define Revueltas's political positions. While most of the short fiction is philosophical in a general, non-systematic sense, it does not address such central political-philosophical questions as existentialism versus marxism, and orthodoxy versus revisionism. In the final analysis, therefore, it may be safely stated that Revueltas's novels provided him with a forum and an outlet for his political concerns, while his short stories satisfied his needs and preoccupations as an artist. Since Revueltas's short fiction did not require a political orientation, it attracted a large readership. Both Party and non-Party critics were able to pass favorable judgment on his short stories while simultaneously condemning his novels. So conspicuous was this phenomenon that Evodio Escalante suspects these same literary critics of purposely promoting Revueltas's short stories as a means to detract from his novels.7

Significantly, Revueltas's first and last pieces of fiction were short stories. His production included over forty such works written from 1937 to 1971. Most of the stories appeared originally in literary journals and newspapers, although some are yet to be published. During Revueltas's lifetime, he published his most significant stories in three collections, which are discussed in this study: Dios en la tierra, (God on Earth, 1944); Dormir en tierra, (To Sleep on Earth, 1960); and Material de los sueños, (Dream Matter, 1973). A fourth collection, titled Las cenizas (Ashes), was published posthumously in 1981 and contains all of Revueltas's stories, both published and unpublished, not included in the three previous collections.8 Unfortunately, Ashes was not available in time for inclusion in this study. These collections, spanning some four decades, reflect an evolving narrative art that was audacious, innovative, and uncompromising. When studied as a whole, there emerge three identifiable stages in the evolution of Revueltas's short fiction: from 1937 to 1947, the cultivation of an artistic story utilizing experimental narrative techniques; from 1953 to 1965, a shift to a more traditional narrative mode;

and from 1969 to 1971, an abstract story
incorporating elements of pure philosophy. These
three stages were intimately linked to developments
in Revueltas's personal and political life.

God on Earth   (1944)

The publication of God on Earth followed one
year after the highly acclaimed The Stone Knife.
In fact, it may be assumed that the success of the
award-winning novel played a key role in affording
Revueltas the opportunity to publish his first
collection of short stories, for he was by then an
established author.   In spite of his reputation,
however, critics initially paid scant attention to the
work.   Even though God on Earth would eventually
prove to be a benchmark in Mexican literature, its
very experimental nature and modernity went
unnoticed at first.

Two critics did respond, however, one negatively
and the other with guarded optimism.   Shortly
after its publication, God on Earth was attacked
with vigor by Antonio Sánchez Barbudo.   Finding
virtually nothing redeeming in the collection, the
Spanish critic asserted: "Revueltas's great defect,
what obscures his work to the point of making it
impenetrable, lacking in interest for the reader,
lacking in value as a realized work of art, is his
absence of craftsmanship, of refinement, of
order."9   Sánchez Barbudo's commentary, however,
not only failed to assess critically the quality of
God on Earth, but exposed the critic's general lack
of appreciation for the modern short story.
Apparently the lack of clear form and structure in
the various stories baffled the commentator.
Several weeks later, Alí Chumacero reviewed the

work and indicated an awareness, at least, that
Revueltas's short stories were new and different;
Chumacero's critical eye seemed to grasp the
importance of <u>God on Earth</u>, and, importantly, he
was neither disturbed nor distracted by the stories'
lack of plot, time shifts, and amorphous nature: "A
superhuman force transcends his (Revueltas's)
stories as if borne from the upper regions of space
or from some unknown god who suddenly introduces
himself into one of the characters without taking
into account the latter's will."[10] Thus Chumacero
intuited the now hallowed critical opinion of <u>God
on Earth</u>; the work is today unanimously acclaimed
for its literary quality and its historical
significance in Mexican literature.

<u>God on Earth</u> includes sixteen stories written
between 1938 and 1944, all but two of which were
initially published in Mexican journals and
newspapers.[11] Taken as a whole, the stories may
be characterized as subjective, poetic, intense,
abstract, and psychologically probing. Language
and style subsume plot and action, relegating the
latter to minimal importance. Fundamental to all
the stories is an attempt to forge an artistically
disquieting but superior work. They are consonant
with European and North American short fiction of
the time, but influenced by specific Mexican
writers, perhaps most noticeably by Efrén
Hernández. Timothy Murad has succinctly stated
both the importance and essence of the collection:
"In contrast to the colloquial and somewhat prosaic
style of the story of the Revolution, the style of
stories of <u>God on Earth</u> is intense and unrelenting,
sustained by the careful repetition of images and
objects. Style lies at the heart of the creation of
atmosphere which is a hallmark of the <u>cuentos</u> of
the volume. Atmosphere becomes the emotive and

artistic framework in which the stories unfold and characters move."[12]   To achieve singular impact and vision in each story, Revueltas utilized an omniscient narrator, suppressed plot and dialogue, chose extreme situations for his characters, and firmly placed the limited action within a highly sculpted, hermetic, and almost static environment. As if testing his characters, he submitted them to pain and agony, violence and perversion, incarceration and despair, and sickness and death. The characters in God on Earth, although purposely ill-defined and underdeveloped, are Revueltas's countrymen who, by and large, live on the margins of society and are engaged in a desperate existential struggle with daily life.   Their confrontations with reality result in an existential denuding whereby they are placed defenselessly on the ragged edges of human existence.   The central conflicts portrayed evidence a generous variety of themes and conditions, many of which were cultivated in the novels.   In the final analysis it is the thematic differentiation, rather than similarities, that strikes the reader of God on Earth with a narrative richness.   Thus any notion of formulating connecting threads, common organizing principles, or analogous structural patterns effectually falsifies the kaleidoscopic nature of the collection.

God on Earth begins and ends with stories set during the War of the Christers (1926-1929); the historical framework, however, is of little or no importance in the narrations.   The first of the works, "God on Earth," gives its title to the entire collection and has come to be a symbolic model of Revueltas's short stories.   Its setting is unspecified, but is in and around a small village presumably in the rural regions of Mexico.   A contingent of government troops in search of drinking water approaches the outskirts of the town, hoping to rendezvous with a local schoolteacher who has previously promised to lead them to water. In aiding the federal troops the schoolteacher commits an act of treason in the eyes of his fellow townsmen. The latter, portrayed as fanatical and vengeful Christers, mete out their retribution by murdering the traitor through impalement.

The simplicity of "God on Earth" with regard to anecdote is a good example of Revueltas's reductive approach to surface action and surface meaning. The story is, in fact, a rich and complex commentary on man's inhumanity, the cultural role of religion in society, and one of the most tragic moments in Mexican history. At work are numerous artistic devices and techniques that Revueltas employed consistently in his short fiction. The characters are effectively muted through the use of an omniscient narrator. Time and space are obscured, lineal structure is juxtaposed, and language inclines toward the poetical and emotive. The result is that the reader must cautiously decipher and extrapolate meanings through symbols and metaphors in much the same way that one reads poetry. This is no easy task, and, as Luis Leal points out, "it is almost always necessary to read Revueltas' short stories twice."[13] In brief, nothing is readily apparent, least of all the author's intention.

"¿Cuánta será la oscuridad?" (How Great Is That Darkness?) also takes as its setting the War of the Christers. The biblical title (Matthew 6:23) assumes significance at both anecdotal and symbolic levels. A group of Mexican Protestants has been attacked and tortured by a roving band of Christers. After suffering humiliation and physical abuse the Protestants flee to the desert to hide from their pursuers. Experiencing mass fear and confusion, the frightened flock looks to its pastor for spiritual guidance and physical protection. The latter, whose eyeglasses were forcibly taken from him by the Christers during the previous skirmish, is unable to respond to the needs of his followers. Rather, he cowers in fear. As his faith and strength are neutralized, he finally goes completely blind.

As in the case of "God on Earth," "How Great Is That Darkness?" is also an artistic exposition on hatred and inhumanity. By placing his central themes within the historical context of the War of the Christers, an event whose most salient feature was its religious fervor, Revueltas was able to achieve sublime ironies. The use of biblical themes, myth, and symbols, so favored by Revueltas in his novels, is likewise in evidence in many of his short stories. In the latter, the author's adept manipulation of these items is particularly noteworthy. Typical of Revueltas's virtuosity is his use of the human eye as a multifaceted symbol in "How Great Is That Darkness?" By extension, Revueltas creates a tight network of meanings (biblical, psychological, and physical) which relate in various ways to vision: the dichotomy between sight and blindness moves in parallel fashion with spiritual vision and demoralization, and finally with life and death; while vengeance and hatred blind the Christers, they become the eye of God pursuing Cain. Ironically, the blind Christers (who are sighted) blind the minister. The Protestant followers, blinded by fear, seek comfort from a blind leader. Attendant to all of this are the additional literary notions of the eye as a window of the soul and a source of knowledge. Thus, the dizzying potential of just one symbol, necessarily treated here with brevity, illustrates the poetic and philosophic nature of Revueltas's short fiction.

Two stories deal with incarceration. "El quebranto" (The Surrender) was originally written as the first chapter of a novel by the same title (see Chapter 2). Highly autobiographical, the story relates the fears and anxieties of a young boy while he is processed for internment at a reformatory. As in many of Revueltas's stories, a contrapuntal structure is used whereby the action alternates between the present and the past. In this case, the protagonist recalls prior episodes from his school and home as he observes with terror his new surroundings and fellow inmates. The anecdote derives from Revueltas's reformatory experience at the age of fifteen. "The Surrender" lacks the usual intensity of Revueltas's stories, undoubtedly because it was conceived within a novelistic framework. Nevertheless, its unique point of view and its biographical value make it a significant work within Revueltas's literary production.

"La conjetura" (The Escape Plan) is also autobiographical, describing the elaborate plans of two prisoners to escape from the Islas Marías. Carefully weighing the circumstances, Reyes and El Pinto concoct a plan whereby they will stow away on a cargo ship, flee the prison colony, and make their way to freedom. Before implementing the plan, however, they are forced to remove a dying man from the prison compound so that his disease-related odor will not disturb the other prisoners. Initially they believe the man to be suffering from malaria, but when they discover that he has cholera, they are struck with fear and go running through the countryside to escape the dread disease.

Revueltas's hermetic worlds, his singularity of impression, and his penchant for extreme situations (incarceration and death) reinforce each other to project an ephemeral, unreal atmosphere that is grounded in an agonizing realism. Thus the portrait presented in the few pages of "The Escape Plan" tells more about the essence of prison life in the Islas Marías than does the entire novel of Walls of Water. What the short story does not seek to do, of course, is extemporize on politics and political consciousness, topics reserved for Revueltas's novels.

As a rule, Revueltas avoided costumbrismo and indigenismo in his novels and short stories. While in The Stone Knife and Earthly Days the Indian and his culture receive considerable attention, they do not achieve significant thematic proportions. Likewise, in the short stories, only two works may be said to deal with Indians per se, and then not for the purpose of treating their culture. In "Barra de Navidad" the themes of infidelity and revenge are portrayed within the world of an Indian labor camp. The Indians are clearing land for a new highway to Barra de Navidad, a port city in the state of Jalisco. Chuy, the protagonist, returns home in a drunken stupor, only to discover that his wife has been with another man. As a result of the infelicitous discovery, it is tacitly understood that the two men must someday fight to the death. When the confrontation occurs, Chuy mortally wounds his rival with a machete.

"El dios vivo" (The Living God) also treats the world of the Indian. In this case a tribe has allowed some white farmers the use of its land in exchange for a percentage of the harvest. But the farmers have reneged on their promise. The local Indian chief, furious over the deceit, has forbidden his people to attend a party given by the whites. In open defiance of the chief's orders, a member of the tribe does attend and, upon returning home, is resolutely punished for disobeying.

In both "Barra de Navidad" and "The Living God" Revueltas resisted the temptation for social commentary concerning the Indian's plight in Mexico. This was in keeping with Revueltas's tendency to avoid social moralizing in his stories which, in turn, permitted him to devote full energies to creating a truly artistic short story that did not seek to instruct the reader, as did his novels, but rather to elucidate human situations, both commonplace and extraordinary. Thus "Barra de Navidad" and "The Living God" probe not the psychological interior of the Indian, but that of universal man, specifically, his notion of justice and retribution.

Although Revueltas seldom treated politics in any form in his short stories, "El corazón verde" ("The Green Heart") is an exception. The work somewhat cryptically describes two seasoned Party workers in their attempt to stop the closing of a foundry and thus save the jobs of the men in their community. The Party workers, Molotov and El Pescador, prepare a handbill for dissemination in the community calling for the factory workers to resist any effort to close the local foundry. To raise the money necessary to print the handbill they must rely on the good will of a prostitute who herself had maintained contact with the Party for many years. Unfortunately, before the material can be disseminated, the factory is closed. All in all, the story is one of Revueltas's most curious. While dealing with the real issues of unemployment, hunger, and family disintegration, the Communist workers, unlike those of the novels, border on the inept and are completely unable to mount even a project so simple as dissemination of propaganda. Nevertheless, the various components of the story--the central characters, the scenes, and the somewhat confused story line--make for a fascinating story of man's alienation, suffering, and general disorientation in modern society.

"Verde es el color de la esperanza" (Green Is the Color of Hope) also treats the subject of unemployment. The story deals with a minor government office clerk who has lost his job after twenty years of service. Consumed with the apparently unjustified hope of being reappointed to his position, he becomes progressively manic-compulsive while awaiting the arrival of his notification in the mail. While his family suffers from near starvation, he remains resolutely stoic in the face of hunger and solitude. The story is noteworthy for the way in which Revueltas captures the essence of man's resignation in the face of tragedy and despair. The protagonist's unyielding hope is at once both touching and sad.

Death, a recurrent theme in Revueltas's novels, appears as an important theme in most of the short stories in God on Earth. At times it assumes central importance. A particularly stunning example is the very brief "La venadita" (The Deer), in which the author describes the pathetic killing of a mother deer and her fawns. With poetic mastery Revueltas vividly contrasts the innocent and bucolic existence of the deer with the cold and calculating advances of the hunters. While the anecdote is not particularly original, its treatment is, underlining the author's virtuosity as a creator of the artistic short story. Filled with brooding symbols and metaphors, Revueltas's "The Deer" engulfs the reader in a commonplace situation and proceeds to metamorphize it into an almost surreal episode.

In "Preferencias" (Preferences) death also occupies center stage. With the help of her neighbors, a woman gives birth to a son. After the newborn cries all night and into the following day, a neighbor lady finally decides to investigate. Upon entering the home she discovers that the mother has died. The neighbors take up a collection and afford her a decent burial. Several days after the mother's funeral the same neighbors suddenly realize that the newborn infant has stopped crying. Rushing to the child's house they discover that he too had died from hunger, since no one had fed him since his mother's death.

Yet another treatment of death is found in "Una mujer en la tierra" (A Woman on Earth). Utilizing an almost uncanny mixture of biblical and allegorical language, Revueltas investigates the nature of life and death and their metaphysical interdependence. By projecting multiple images whose components are primary forces in the universe--earth, sky, air, and organic matter--the reader is necessarily carried to the very dividing line between life and death, existence and nonexistence. "A Woman on Earth" must rate as one of Revueltas's most intense and philosophical short stories.

Revueltas's tendency to place his characters in stressful situations in order to examine man in the light of tragedy and despair accounts for the high incidence of physical and mental disorders so prevalent in his novels and his short stories. The former recall such exceptional cases as the epileptic Temblorino, in <u>Walls of Water</u>, the one-eyed Tuerto Ventura in <u>Earthly Days</u>, the psychologically disturbed landowner in <u>In Some Valley of Tears</u>, and the physically wretched El Carajo in <u>Isolation Cell</u>. Likewise, the short stories evidence the same preoccupation with such disorders, and, as in the novels, they range from the commonplace to the bizarre and the grotesque.

In addition to the blind minister in "How Great Is That Darkness?" and the cholera-ridden Amarillo in "The Escape Plan," other stories also focus considerable attention on physical and mental disorders. "La acusación" (The Accusation), for instance, deals with the case of Cristóbal, a young man who is attacked by a swarm of bees. As a result of the experience he loses an eye and is forced to wear an ill-fitted glass eye as a substitute. Shunned by the superstitious people of his village, he is accused of being the embodiment of evil. Finally, he is murdered by the townspeople to rid themselves of their misfortunes. Bordering on the grotesque, Cristóbal's condition is a pretext for the author's statement of man's intolerance for those whose physical features radically deviate from the norm.

In "El abismo" (The Abyss) Revueltas fuses mental and physical disorders in the form of alcoholism. Martínez, an office worker, suffers from the boredom and meaninglessness of life. Seemingly trapped, he turns to alcohol for escape; progressively he falls into the clutches of alcoholism and eventually begins to suffer from blackouts. Shortly after one such episode, Martínez's fellow workers maliciously convince him that, during a drunken stupor, he has killed a man. Martínez, believing the cruel hoax, is struck with fear and awaits the arrival of the police at his office. Giving way to paranoia, however, he pathetically tries to escape. In an effort to disguise himself he borrows some clothes from one of the joke's perpetrators. Purposely trying to carry the hoax to new heights, the latter gives Martínez clothes that do not fit him. Thus, as Martínez, looking perfectly ridiculous, exits from the office, his colleagues laugh uproariously. But Martínez is unaware of any of this and emotionally thanks the man for helping him escape.

The ravaging effects of chronic illness are treated in "El hijo tonto" (The Idiot). A bedridden mother and her retarded son are the two principals in this pessimistic tale of delirium and despair. Suffering from an unspecified disease, the mother anguishes through a cold and rainy night, anxiously awaiting the arrival of daylight. In her desperation she convinces herself that the sunlight of the new day will bring a new state of well-being and strength. Her false hopes, produced by her delirium, are moderated by the presence of her awkward son, whose actions drive her to a point of irrational hostility. Unable to contain her anxiety she sends her child outside to see if the sun has begun to shine. When the boy reports to her that it is in fact still raining, she cannot accept the truth and attributes the bad news to her son's ineptness. Finally, she transcends her predicament by imagining that she sees a small ray of sunlight through the window.

In addition to mental and physical disorders, Revueltas was interested in man's philosophical malaise. One of the author's best examples of man's existential trauma is found in "La soledad" (Solitude). The protagonist, a kind of government ombudsman attached to a police precinct, is overwhelmed with the meaninglessness and futility of life. The reader observes him at work during a murder investigation which, as it turns out, was really a suicide. "Solitude," like most of the stories in God on Earth, contains little surface action and, hence, sparse surface meaning. Rather, the work is a complex morass of philosophical speculations on life and death in the modern age.

In "La caída" (The Fall) Revueltas brings together a large number of previously discussed thematic elements to produce one of his strangest tales. Utilizing various reference points (different times and locales) which flow into a careful mix, the reader is afforded a multi-dimensional view of Eusebio, the mentally deranged protagonist. Having had incestuous relations with his sister, Eusebio has become assailed by feelings of guilt. As a means to atone for his sins, he strangely arrives at the decision to have his feet amputated, since it was with these that he had so often caressed his sister. A doctor friend, however, succeeds in dissuading him. Eusebio's strange mental and emotional problems are exacerbated by his alcoholism. Revueltas reflects the protagonist's mental disarray through the general disorienting effect of the narration in which the reader proceeds with uncertainty about cause and effect, time line, and, indeed, even the verity of numerous actions described by the omniscient narrator. The result is a tour de force of short fiction.

To Sleep on Earth (1960)

Consisting of eight works written between 1945 and 1958 Dormir en tierra (To Sleep on Earth) is, for many, Revueltas's best single collection of short fiction. Several of its stories are generally accepted as true classics of Mexican literature.

Two of the works, "To Sleep on Earth," which gives its name to the entire collection, and "La palabra sagrada" (The Sacred Word), have moved the Mexican critic Jaime Labastida to proclaim them as the "best two short stories that, until now, have ever been written in this country."14 But it is the collection as a whole that has captured critical acclaim. For José Agustín, To Sleep on Earth is "the best book of short stories that has been written in Mexico."15 By any measurement, it is a milestone in Latin American short fiction.

The collection was originally conceived by Revueltas in 1953; it was to include six stories and was to be titled "La frontera increíble." For unknown reasons Revueltas was unable to secure its publication and waited until 1960, when, with the addition of two more stories, the collection was finally published. Five of the works were written in the 1940s: "La frontera increíble," "Lo que sólo uno eschucha. . . ," "Los hombres en el pantano," "Noche de epifanía," and "La hermana enemiga." In many ways, they represent an immediate and natural extension of the short fiction included in God on Earth. Three stories, however, were written in the 1950s and exhibit marked differences from their predecessors. Thus, To Sleep on Earth is important because it represents a point of transition in the evolution of Revueltas's narrative produced both before and after the literary polemics occasioned by Earthly Days and Quadrant of Solitude (see Chapters 2 and 4). Critical evaluations that characterize the collection as unified and harmonious do so at the risk of misrepresenting the nature of To Sleep on Earth. A judicious appraisal of the collection must recognize the radical and dramatic shift in style and technique observable between the earlier stories of the 1940s and those of the 1950s. Specifically, the later stories display a decided movement away from the earlier amorphous, plotless, and actionless works in favor of a more traditional, surface-action story with a clear and logical plot. In addition, there is a drift toward a coherent, chronological time line, moderating the earlier propensity for major disruptions and juxtapositions of time elements. Finally, language becomes less connotative in the later works, producing a less poetic but more exacting narrative. As a logical consequence of these changes, more fully developed and less perplexing characters emerge.

It is also possible to differentiate the thematic concerns treated by Revueltas in the 1940s as opposed to the 1950s. The earlier works in To Sleep on Earth are clearly extensions and elaborations of those themes and concerns treated in God on Earth, and the stories represent some of the best examples of Revueltas's most fully blossomed existentialist fiction. On the other hand, the stories written after 1950 display a marked gravitation away from such tendencies and themes, and a movement toward an objectified examination of society. This change, more so than those of technique, was prompted by Revueltas's relationship with the Mexican Communist party during the 1950s. Yet even with an obvious attempt to please Party critics, Revueltas could not entirely abandon his existentialist concerns. Thus, it is not surprising that To Sleep on Earth was not published until after Revueltas's second expulsion from the Party.

Several stories in To Sleep on Earth are direct descendants of the artistic story cultivated in God on Earth. A good example is "La frontera increíble" (The Incredible Frontier), which investigates the perennially fascinating dividing line between life and death. The nearly actionless plot treats the final moments of a dying man as he is observed by his immediate family. Action, dialogue, character development, and setting are suppressed so that Revueltas may focus on the psychological state of the dying protagonist. In doing so, there emerges an eerie commentary on man's solitude and his inability to communicate with the living. There is a clear suggestion that only through death can man truly comprehend his earthly reality. When the protagonist, in his last moments, reaches a transcendental and revelatory state, he faces his death unable to communicate either the experiential or existential revelations of the event. In attempting to capture the essence of man's passage from life to death, Revueltas not only obscures the boundary between the two, but he posits a demonic inversion in which life is death, and vice versa.[16]

Another story, "Lo que sólo uno escucha". . . (What Only One Man Hears . . .), is similar in theme to "The Incredible Frontier." In fact, the story was originally titled "La frontera increíble" but was subsequently renamed.[17] With considerable ambiguity, it relates an episode in the pathetic life of a lackluster violinist who, while alone one day at home, manages to play a sonata with, he believes, absolute mastery. Apparently overcome by the beauty of his musical execution, the protagonist enters into a state of wonderment. But extenuating circumstances soon lead the reader to question the musician's judgment. It is revealed that the protagonist has a drinking problem and, in fact, is on the verge of death. Thus the episode, which is related by an omniscient narrator, is under suspicion given the uncertain state of the protagonist, since the latter's stupefaction has plausible sources other than his music. The violinist's wife, on the other hand, provides a counterpoint to her husband's confused and euphoric state. She is an objective observer who clearly sees that her husband is dying, and she proceeds to comfort him in his final moment. The musician, as with the case of the dying man in "The Incredible Frontier," enters a revelatory state in which he previews his passage from life to death, coupled with the devastating realization that he cannot effectively communicate his experience to his loved ones. In effect, his impending death permits him to grasp the true nature of human solitude.

Two stories in To Sleep on Earth, "Los hombres en el pantano" (The Men in the Swamp) and "Noche de epifanía" (Night of Epiphany), have international settings and occur during World War II. Both factors make them unique among Revueltas's short fiction. While the former reveals the author's inclination to move away from a purely Mexican setting, the latter points to Revueltas's passionate hatred of fascism, projected in an exaggerated manner as the result of his commitment to Marxism. While Revueltas's short stories tend to be both ahistorical and apolitical, these two works are exceptions.

A South Pacific island provides the setting for "The Men in the Swamp." It describes a frightening nighttime confrontation between an American military patrol and its Japanese counterpart. As the narration begins, three sleepless days and nights have passed with the soldiers standing chest-deep in water. Both groups are forced to remain silent and motionless lest they reveal their positions to each other. The scene, through the use of an omniscient narrator, is viewed through the eyes and thoughts of Joe Martínez, a Chicano soldier from Texas. As Martínez speculates on the desperate situation, an American soldier is heard moving in the dark. Martínez realizes that the soldier will soon be set upon by enemy troops. As he awaits the ensuing encounter, Martínez concludes that the American is Smith, a black Texan in his patrol. Suddenly Martínez hears the unmistakable sounds of hand-to-hand combat, culminating in the death of the American. At the story's end Martínez shockingly discovers that the victim is not Smith, but Martínez's own brother-in-law.

"The Men in the Swamp" is one of Revueltas's least impressive stories. The action, presumably meant to be realistic, is entirely unconvincing, and the surprise ending is less than satisfactory. The exclusive use of blacks and Chicanos to portray the American force reveals a naive Marxist prejudice. In spite of these defects, the story is an earnest attempt to explore the existential implications of war. The soldiers, suffering from hunger, cold, physical exhaustion, and sensory deprivation, are placed at the very edge of reality. The ambience, consisting of a fusion of nature and the necessities of war, is the story's organizing principle.

"Night of Epiphany" is set in an undisclosed European city. The story's psychological backdrop is one of terror provided by the constant threat of German air raids. The plot deals with a Jewish couple, Rebeca and Isaac, whose marriage is breaking up. Rebeca concludes that if her husband were to have spontaneous sexual relations with another woman, he might once again love her, Rebeca. The pretext for the story's action occurs when Rebeca and Isaac accidentally meet on a stairway in complete darkness. Although Rebeca recognizes Isaac, he takes her for a stranger. When he makes sexual advances toward her she decides to comply. At that point Isaac discovers her true identity and, enraged, accuses her of unfaithfulness and promptly kills her. Police arrive at the scene of the crime and remove Rebeca's body to the morgue, where she is prepared for cremation. The story ends with Isaac requesting to see his wife's corpse one last time.

Various themes and techniques common to Revueltas's early literature are employed in "Night of Epiphany." Biblical references abound, there is considerable play with the time line, and there are strange and perplexing characters such as a lesbian nurse and a sexually frustrated clergyman. As in the case of "The Men in the Swamp," Revueltas casts the action in nearly complete darkness to effect an eerie atmosphere calculated to underscore the terror and panic of war. The characters, having suffered the persistent threat of air raids, reflect an ennui that suggests a meaninglessness in life. The breakdown of normal social patterns has led to gratuitous sex. Violence and death have been integrated into the characters' existence to such a point that they have forgotten that men die for reasons other than war. Thus, when Rebeca dies at the hands of her husband, it is as if the characters regain some of their lost humanity through the victim's demise; furthermore, they appear to experience a moment of epiphany, as the title suggests.

"La hermana enemiga" (The Hostile Sister) is an intense psychological exploration of sibling rivalry. But as Timothy Murad points out, the story is much more than simply a case study: "Rich in imagery and cumulative in the tonal force of its language, the story goes beyond realistic detail to achieve symbolic import."[18] Two stepsisters, one clever and malicious and the other naive and innocent, are the central characters. The older, hateful stepsister, through a series of actions calculated to embarrass, discredit, and hurt her younger sibling, succeeds in driving the innocent girl to commit suicide. Prior to dying, the young girl suffers repeated indignities, including physical abuse, slander, and overwhelming guilt complexes maliciously induced by her stepsister. Atmosphere and psychical-spiritual elements take precedence over both plot and character development. The tension between the two girls is masterfully narrated by Revueltas, producing one of his best and most unusual tales.

The remaining three stories in To Sleep on Earth, all written in the 1950s, reflect the already discussed shift in style, technique, and theme that marks them from the earlier works. The three works in question, all highly significant examples of Mexican short fiction, account for Fernando Díez's critical comments concerning the narrative found in God on Earth as opposed to "some" of the works found in To Sleep on Earth: "Revueltas goes, in a certain sense, from the obscure to the evident, from the subjective to the objective, from the abstract to the concrete, although this switch is perceptible in only some of the stories."[19] Díez's remarks, while not applicable to the earlier works of To Sleep on Earth, aptly capture the essence of "The Sacred World," "The Language of the Dispossessed," and "To Sleep on Earth."

"The Sacred Word" involves the cover-up of an incident in which Alicia, a sixteen-year-old student, and her boyfriend are discovered by a teacher in the school attic while they are engaged in sex.

For unexplained reasons, the teacher is disposed to conceal the students' indiscretion and, in doing so, assumes the blame for having sexually molested Alicia.[20] The young girl quickly seizes upon the opportunity to play the role of innocent victim and, when she is taken to bed, proceeds cynically and maliciously to weep and moan. As her father, her school principal, and a nurse try to comfort her, Alicia hides her contempt for them, relishing her newfound role as object of their concern. The story relates Alicia's secret thoughts and memories as she lies in bed. In particular, she recalls how her Aunt Ene, years earlier, had falsely assumed the role of a wailing mourner upon the death of her husband. It is not without reason, therefore, that Aunt Ene, at the close of the story, approaches Alicia's bedside and whispers that she, Ene, is fully aware of her niece's guilt and false lament.

"The Sacred Word" contains many elements used by Revueltas in his earlier stories, most notably a considerable play with time and an omniscient narrator. But at least two things are new. There is a coherent plot line with numerous episodes connected by cause-and-effect relationships. In addition, the story is, in large part, a social commentary which criticizes bourgeois values. Thus "The Sacred Word" represents a turning point in Revueltas's short fiction in that it is primarily a social critique (from a Marxist perspective) constructed within a relatively traditional framework. Emphasis is given to the coordination of temporal and spatial elements to achieve an explication of reality, at the expense of the earlier tendency of centering the story around the concerns and sufferings of an individual.[21] In spite of the fact that the story is narrated exclusively from Alicia's point of view, there emerge two distinct points of view concerning the incident at school: Alicia's informed notion of reality, versus the ill-informed and hypocritical view shared by her father and others who represent the bourgeoisie.

The drift away from the earlier artistic short story to a more traditional one is even more apparent in "El lenguaje de nadie" (The Language of the Dispossessed). It is reminiscent of In Some Valley of Tears, which was written in the same year. The protagonist, Carmelo, is a destitute Indian who works for Doña Quilina, a malicious and miserly owner of a sizable hacienda. Impoverished and struggling for his very existence, Carmelo pleads with Doña Quilina to rent him a rocky, infertile section of land, thinking that she will surely grant such a meager request. The landowner, however, refuses. She cannot believe anyone would be interested in the unproductive plot and suspects the Indian of ulterior motives. Meanwhile, a typhus epidemic breaks out. When Doña Quilina falls victim to the disease, she is attended to in her dying moments by Carmelo and his companion, Tiliches, a pathetically deformed deaf-mute. The two men, mistakenly believing their landlady to be dead, carry her to the cemetery, where, before the actual interment, noises are heard coming from her coffin. Terrified by the incident, Tiliches runs away, but Carmelo superstitiously believes that the dead woman is simply trying to scare him, and he completes the burial. Unbeknownst to the poor Indian, he has been named by Doña Quilina as the sole benefactor of her estate. Her relatives, outraged and resentful, enter into collusion with a local judge and accuse Carmelo of having buried the landowner alive. They promise to forget the whole matter, however, if he signs a document waiving his rights to a "little piece of land."   Carmelo, frightened and confused, gratefully signs the paper and returns to his hut with an inexplicable feeling of loss.

"The Language of the Dispossessed" is conventional in virtually every respect. The narrator, with denotative, realistic language, re-creates a thoroughly traditional setting in rural Mexico populated with believable characters. The plot is clear and it proceeds chronologically. The story shows with certainty that Revueltas had abandoned, at least temporarily, his earlier amorphous short fiction in favor of surface action. Thematically the work interweaves two concerns: class conflict and philosophical speculation on the nature of language.   In the former, Revueltas unleashes a rigorous attack on the greed, corruption, and the lack of compassion of Mexico's bourgeoisie. Doña Quilina, her relatives, and the judge represent the power elite that runs roughshod over the poor.   In dialectical opposition to them are Carmelo and Tiliches; they embody the principle of the second theme, language, in that theirs is the language of nadie, the poor, the alienated, and the dispossessed.   Carmelo can communicate with his deaf-mute friend, Tiliches, but he is baffled by the bourgeoisie's language, and they simply cannot understand him.   Revueltas posits a powerful statement concerning the social, economic, and political nature of language in society.[22]

"To Sleep on Earth," written in 1958, is chronologically the last work in the collection. It is divided into three distinct segments that proceed lineally and thread the action. The first episode begins in a Mexican port; Revueltas paints the sordid life of prostitutes and unemployed dockworkers. Of central interest are La Chunca, a haggard and pathetic prostitute, and her young son. La Chunca, wanting a better life for her son, but unable to escape the clutches of prostitution, seeks to give custody of the boy to any party that will take him. The second episode occurs at the city's dockside where Galindo, the chief petty officer of the Tritón, a cargo ship, is frantically overseeing loading operations. In a desperate act, La Chunca goes to the dock and beseeches Galindo to take her son with him to Veracruz. She has little to offer but a small amount of money and her body. Galindo categorically refuses and, shortly thereafter, the ship departs. In the third episode the Tritón runs headlong into a cyclone and sinks. Prior to the tragedy, Galindo discovers that the young boy has stowed away on board. In an effort to save the boy's life, Galindo, a truly decent man, forces the boy into a life jacket and throws him overboard. As the story ends, the boy, the only survivor of the disaster, indicts Galindo for having cruelly thrown him into the sea.

"To Sleep on Earth" is a classic of contemporary Mexican short fiction. Jaime Labastida considers it to be "a key short story in Mexican literature; it may be said that it is a milestone in the history of our literature."23 That the work has garnered such a reputation is interesting since it is completely traditional in structure and technique. Additionally, it is nearly devoid of social commentary. Thus it is generally outside the confines of most of Revueltas's short fiction. Nevertheless, its great strength as an example of solid storytelling has assured it a position in Mexican literature. Action and human interest completely subsume the issues of alienation and death. Although the latter two themes are

present in abundance, the importance of "To Sleep
on Earth" within the context of Revueltas's fiction
is precisely the manner in which he opted for a
structured anecdote as opposed to philosophical
speculations. Galindo's heroic act at the end of
the story, for instance, completely overshadows the
implicit presentation of the theme of human
solitude as relates to his life as an abandoned
lover. In short, by 1958 Revueltas was producing a
new fiction which was, ironically, a return to an
older and more traditional narrative.

Dream Matter (1974)

Material de los sueños (Dream Matter),
Revueltas's last short-story collection published
during his lifetime, contains six of the author's best
short stories plus a cluster of four vignettes.
Three of the short stories were written in 1965 and
represent a continuation of the more traditional
narrative cultivated by Revueltas in the 1950s.
Their basically conventional format was not the
result of political courtship, however, as in the
case of their predecessors, but rather of
Revueltas's preferred style at the time. Three of
the stories were written during his imprisonment in
Lecumberri and mark a radical departure from the
author's previous short fiction in virtually every
respect. Therefore, Dream Matter, like To Sleep
on Earth, bridges two distinct periods in the
evolution of Revueltas's short fiction. In short, it
includes some of his best examples of traditional
narrative, as well as a new, highly abstract,
enigmatic literature based on or at least
incorporating elements of philosophy ranging from
Hegel to Sartre.

Dream Matter has not enjoyed the same critical acclaim as have Revueltas's previous collections. José de la Colina, however, has lauded the collection as "visions in which the charged tension of his (Revueltas's) observing eye, his burning intelligence for detecting meaningful images, for discovering the point of maximum opacity or of fulguration in the story that reality seeks to tell us, all come together in verbal music, in a dark canto filled with lightning."24   While some critics have sought to ascribe a unifying theme to the collection, such a notion is generally inaccurate. Dream Matter simply brought together Revueltas's short stories written after the publication of To Sleep on Earth, irrespective of content or technique.   The collection's very diversity defies attempts at homogenizing its works.

"Dream Matter," which gives its name to the collection, consists of four separately titled vignettes: "Virgo," "El sino del escorpión" (The Scorpion's Fate), "La multiplicación de los peces" (The Multiplication of the Fish) and "Nocturno en que todo se oye" (A Nocturne in Which All Is Heard).   Of the four pieces, only "Virgo" resembles a short story because of its anecdote: a protagonist narrator recalls an incident in the city of Poza Rica, where he went to a brothel and slept with a prostitute.   Suggesting little more than a writing exercise, "Virgo" appears to be related to Revueltas's more traditional narrative in that it coherently recounts a simple event with little recourse to symbols, connotative language, and so forth.   But its very scarcity of action, climax, and moral places it outside traditional short-story narration.

"The Scorpion's Fate" is an ambiguous sketch that personifies the scorpion and speculates on his relationship to man. Opening itself to multiple interpretations, the work is a brief exposition, presumably on the inadequacy of human communication, inhumanity, and misunderstanding. Written shortly after his expulsion from the PCM and the Liga Leninista Espartaco, it is not unreasonable to assume that Revueltas, the true Marxist, was shunned or destroyed in much the way scorpions are.

Both "The Multiplication of the Fish" and "A Nocturne in Which All Is Heard" are introspective vignettes that suggest dream sequences. Filled with enigmatic images, symbols, and metaphors, they are little more than brief impressions devoid of plot, structure, or anecdote. Various elements in the two selections anticipate the abstract narrations that Revueltas cultivated during his stay in Lecumberri some ten years later. Nevertheless, because of their brevity, lack of form, and technique, the pieces that make up "Dream Matter" stand separately from the other works in the collection. José de la Colina has observed that in "Dream Matter" one can say that digression has overpowered all narrative space, that it deals with pure digressions, enclosed within themselves: "Revueltas's imagination has been released, propelling itself to a serene, rhythmic freedom."[25]

The traditional short fiction that Revueltas had turned to in the 1950s as a means to conform his literature to Party norms produced an action-oriented story with a defined anecdote. In 1965, no longer a Party member or courting membership, Revueltas wrote three short stories that, nevertheless, are reminiscent of works like "To Sleep on Earth" and "The Sacred Word." Of the three works, "Sinfonía pastoral" (Pastoral

Symphony) perhaps best illustrates Revueltas's powers as a traditional storyteller.

"Pastoral Symphony" is fundamentally a suspense story with a commentary on bourgeois values. The plot deals with a married couple's duplicity and complicity in the murder of the wife's lover. The action begins at the couple's home, where the wife and lover are alone. When the husband returns home unexpectedly, the lover hides in a large freezer which the husband, indicating no awareness of his wife's deceit, inexplicably locks with a key. The wife, fearful and dismayed, suspects her husband of locking the freezer in a deliberate attempt to trap her lover, but she is not totally convinced, since her mate exhibits no apparent knowledge of the other man's presence. Acting upon the husband's suggestion, the couple then goes to a movie. Afterwards, the husband suddenly suggests that they go for a ride in the country before returning home. During their long absence from the house, the wife struggles to conceal her concern for the lover, who if not soon released from the freezer will face certain death. As the hours pass, she repeatedly, but unsuccessfully, tries to determine whether her husband is acting deliberately or fortuitously. When they finally return home, the wife, through a pretense obtains the key to the freezer from her husband as he goes off to bed. When she goes to release her lover, the husband suddenly reappears and orders her not to open the freezer. It now becomes apparent to the wife that her husband has known about her lover's plight throughout the evening. Without discussing the matter, they retire to bed, leaving the body to be taken for that of a robber when discovered by the cook in the morning.

Several impressive stylistic and technical effects appear in "Pastoral Symphony." For example, tension and suspense are masterfully achieved through Revueltas's manipulation of time with which he stretches minutes and hours into an eternity. Also noteworthy is the clever way in which the action in a movie version of Gide's Pastoral Symphony is interlaced with the primary action of the story. But taken as a whole, Revueltas's "Pastoral Symphony" is noteworthy for its denunciation of Mexican bourgeois values. As Ruffinelli observes, the story's pivotal point is "bourgeois hypocrisy, a hypocrisy based on corroded values whose healthy appearance must be conserved for class interests."[26]

"Resurrección sin vida" (Resurrection without Life), written only one year after Errors, treats the issue of Party loyalty and obedience. The action occurs during World War II, shortly before Hitler's attack on the Soviet Union in 1941. The protagonist, Antelmo Suárez, and his girl friend, Alejandra, are covert agents operating in Cuba under the direction of an unspecified, clandestine, Soviet organization. They are unhappy with their work, however, and plot to escape to another country. Their plans are frustrated when it is discovered that Alejandra has given information to the enemy. Antelmo, acting upon orders from his superiors, murders his girl friend and is then promptly sent to Mexico as a saboteur. Operating out of Mexicali, on the Mexican-U.S. border, his mission is to derail American trains carrying war materiel destined for Europe to be used against the Axis Powers, but after sabotaging only one train he is suddenly ordered to cease his activities. Aware that the new orders anticipate a shift in Soviet alliances from the Axis Powers to the Allies, he becomes frustrated by the capriciousness of international politics and his senseless murder of Alejandra. Provoked to question his blind obedience to his political cause, he is plunged into a crisis of conscience and succumbs to alcoholism. When his despair reaches a breaking point, he attempts suicide but is saved from certain death by the timely intervention of Raquel, his Mexican girl friend.

"Resurrection without Life" is an existentialist drama grounded concretely in history and politics. The latter's thematic presence, rather uncommon in Revueltas's short fiction but so prevalent in his novels, suggests a mini-treatise on the evils of Stalinism not unlike that found in Errors. Luis Arturo Ramos, in commenting on the protagonist's loss of political faith and purpose, observes that the work "is a story of frustration, of deception that is occasioned by an ideal that can never be realized, of death in life that is brought about by fulfilling a responsibility that is imposed upon us. . . ."[27] "Resurrection without Life" was to be the last time that Revueltas would treat the theme of the disillusioned Party worker.

The traditional narrative mode that Revueltas evolved in the 1950s is also present in "Cama 11, un relato autobiográfico" (Bed No. 11, An Autobiographical Sketch). Somewhat similar in structure to "The Sacred Word," the story relates the experiences and recollections of a hospital patient confined to bed. Narrated in the first person by the protagonist, the action alternates between the present and the past. The former includes descriptions of hospital employees, other patients, physical surroundings, and various medical examinations to which the protagonist is subjected. The past is related by means of two major

flashbacks: a conscious recollection dealing with the
adventures of the narrator's former girl friend, and
a dreamlike episode that relates the surreal
massacre of a group of madmen. This last
flashback is notable for its literary craftsmanship;
it is one of the few pieces of Revueltas's literature
to be translated to English.[28] The fragment is
also significant because it seems to anticipate
Revueltas's later story titled "Ezekiel, or The
Massacre of the Innocents."

"Bed No. 11" possesses numerous interesting
stylistic and technical elements. Noteworthy is the
rigidly controlled point of view. The language
employed shifts radically from the vernacular to
scientific-medical jargon.[29] An hermetic
atmosphere is attained whereby the patient's
confinement is similar to the prison experiences so
often described in the author's other works. As
the full title indicates, the work has its inspiration
in a personal episode in Revueltas's life.
Throughout the story there is a dynamic tension
present between the narrator's confinement and his
tendency to move back in time to recapture
activity that he is no longer physically able to
experience. Based on recollection, the author fuses
a painful and humiliating present (the medical
examinations) with a dreamlike past.

Between 1969 and 1971, while imprisoned in
Lecumberri, Revueltas wrote three short stories.
Although few in number, they differ so
substantially from his previous stories that they
may well be considered a new and final step in his
short narrative. During his last years, Revueltas
ceased writing fiction almost entirely. The only
major work during and after his final incarceration
was The Isolation Cell. Instead, he turned to
philosophy (both political and nonpolitical) and

began to produce essays. It is not surprising, therefore, that his last short fiction should exhibit the presence of philosophical considerations only hinted at in previous works.

In January 1969, shortly after being sent to Lecumberri Prison, Revueltas finished "El reojo del yo" (Self-spying), in which he displayed a preoccupation with the formal problems of philosophy. The story's only action involves the narrator, who is alone in his prison cell. As he routinely goes about his daily functions, particularly his bodily functions, he is locked in silent discourse with his other self. The protagonist has, in fact, unfolded into two entities: self and other. Through the use of established philosophical terminology, coupled with appropriate capitalization of select nouns, Revueltas stylistically makes clear that his story is based in large part on a formal philosophical issue. The presence of words such as Knowledge, Praxis, and Other points the reader on his way. Involved are such problems as "otherness," "knowledge of self," and subject-object duality. Language and style in "Self-spying" are dense and rich, both calculated to accentuate the intricacies of the "cat and mouse" game that occurs within the narrator's conscious reality. To extrapolate the many diverse speculative meanings of the narration, "Self-spying" requires careful reading, for with this work Revueltas signaled an abandonment of short fiction that was readily apprehended by the average reader.

Later in the same year, Revueltas wrote what may well be his most demanding and enigmatic piece of short fiction, "Ezequiel o la matanza de los inocentes" (Ezekiel, or The Massacre of the Innocents). As already mentioned, the work was anticipated several years earlier in "Bed No. 11,"

where Revueltas as protagonist narrator describes a
scene he envisions during a delirium provoked by
fever.   The connection is suggested at the end of
the sequence in "Bed No. 11" when the author
refers to the massacre of the madmen as "the
massacre of the innocents."[30]   But in spite of
thematic similarities that are suggested between
the two works, "Ezekiel" is very different from the
selection in "Bed No. 11."

Because of the complex nature of its narrative,
"Ezekiel, or The Massacre of the Innocents" does
not surrender itself to a simple plot synopsis.   The
primary action is limited to one central character,
Ezekiel, who is in a watchtower reading a selection
from the book of Ezekiel in the Bible.   While
reading, he gazes through a window at a group of
people in an outside garden.   From the story's first
sentence, the reader is plunged into a vortex of
introspective reflections, philosophical observations,
and cryptic visions.   There is a powerful
apocalyptic tone not unlike that of the Old
Testament, reinforced by biblical quotations and
symbols.   Thus it is not unimaginable to entertain
a "religious" interpretation of the text.   Because of
its ambiguity, however, Revueltas's "Ezekiel"
transcends any one interpretation.   A
political-historical reading, for instance, is entirely
possible.   That the entire work is a thickly veiled
exposition on the 1968 Student Movement in Mexico
and the resultant "Massacre at Tlatelolco" is highly
probable.   In this connection, it is significant to
note that Revueltas dedicated "Ezekiel" to Martín
Dozal, one of the student leaders and a close
colleague of Revueltas.   Time and again throughout
the puzzling narration there are references that
suggest the hostile antagonism between the Mexican
students in 1968 (the innocents) and Mexico's power

elite.

Yet another fruitful view of "Ezekiel" resides in a purely philosophical reading that revolves around a cluster of established philosophical concerns: time and recollection, history, otherness, consciousness, and the subject-object duality. In fact, accompanying notes to the original manuscript suggest that Revueltas's purpose in "Ezekiel" was nothing less than a formal literary exposition on such topics.31 But whatever interpretation or reading is applied to "Ezekiel," the text remains difficult; it virtually overwhelms the reader. Language laden with secretive symbols and metaphors entirely subsumes anecdote to produce a labyrinth of ideas.

"Hegel y yo" (Hegel and I) is a somewhat moderated example of the highly abstract and philosophical short story that Revueltas cultivated late in life.32 After his death it was discovered that the original title of the story was "El caso del Fut."33 A quick review of the author's original outline of the story reveals the ponderous philosophical levels to which Revueltas had soared during his final imprisonment.34 His last narration is immersed in such complex considerations as Hegel's phenomenological notions of memory and recollection.

The primary action in "Hegel and I" is easily summarized. The protagonist has been sentenced to prison for killing a woman. His cellmate, nicknamed Hegel because he was arrested on a street named after the famous German philosopher, is an amputee who has lost both legs as a result of a shoot-out with the police. Unable to walk, Hegel's only means of mobility is a small platform on wheels. The interaction between the two cellmates is limited primarily to conversations, and

a perverse sadomasochistic game in which the
protagonist kicks Hegel's cart around the room
while the latter holds on for dear life. The major
portion of "Hegel and I," however, is devoted to
the protagonist's numerous recollections. As he sits
in his cell he ponders past experiences: an
encounter on a city bus in Panama, a three-month
drunk in Guayaquil, and an incident in a brothel in
Salina Cruz, Mexico. The story ends with a dream
sequence in which the protagonist confuses
Medarda, his lover, with the woman he murdered.

While the primary action in "Hegel and I" is
locked concretely in time (present) and space
(prison), the protagonist's thoughts spend little time
there. In search of the past, he fluctuates readily
between distinctly different time periods and
geographical locales. Revueltas, in an interview
with Adolfo Ortega, described the purpose and
technique of the narrative employed in "Hegel and
I": "There is a new kind of montage. It not only
deals with the alteration of temporal planes, but of
the combination of emotional, emotive, and
temporal planes with simultaneous action."[35]   In
the same interview Revueltas explained how "Hegel
and I" was to form a chapter in a novel that would
consist of a series of short stories thematically
related. Revueltas stressed, at that time, that the
work would not be philosophical in nature. His
disclaimer to the contrary notwithstanding, what
emerges in "Hegel and I" is a veritable avalanche
of philosophical speculations concerning time,
memory, history and reality. The treatment is
punctuated with quotations or paraphrases from the
philosopher Friedrich Hegel, but teasingly attributed
to the character Hegel. The narrator's confusion
between the two is one of many examples in which
Revueltas suggests an intermingling and melding of

people and ideas through associative connections, resulting in the protagonist's uncertain view of things.

Central to "Hegel and I" is the treatment of time and recollection. Pursuing the age-old question of the relationships among memory, recollection, intuition, and image, Revueltas encapsulates within the story a brilliant exposition of the subject. Referring to the central issue of "Hegel and I," Evodio Escalante observes: "It is as if memory no longer manifests itself, as it has until now, in materializations of the recollected. Now we will only know about it (memory) to the extent that it is impossible to translate it to concrete images."[36] That the forgotten defines the recollected is fundamental to Revueltas's thesis, but this very premise in turn invites confusion. The narrator leads the reader on a dizzying voyage that Luis Arturo Ramos cogently describes: "The planes unfold, pluralize, one story generates another; the protagonist searches, he invades the past, pulverizing events. . . ."[37] To achieve all this, Revueltas employed two different narrative languages: one is an agile and direct language that is reserved for the anecdotes, while the other is a dense and complex language that treats the philosophical problems so strongly present in "Hegel and I."

Chapter Four

The Theater

Although José Revueltas was primarily a prose writer, he wrote five theatrical works early in his literary career, only two of which were both performed and published: Israel and El cuadrante de la soledad (Quadrant of Solitude). Another, Pito Pérez en la hoguera (Pito Pérez in a Fix), was staged late in Revueltas's life, but was not published. Two works, Nos esperan en Abril (They'll Be Waiting for Us in Abril) and Los muertos vivirán (The Dead Will Live), were neither performed nor published.[1] Revueltas's attraction to the theater was considerable. As an intellectual and an artist, he held the theater to be basic among man's activities. He believed that "it is born at the same time that man is born."[2] As a committed Marxist–Leninist, Revueltas viewed the stage to be an instrument for political instruction and social change. On a personal level, Rosaura Revueltas's many contacts as a leading actress cannot be discounted as a natural conduit for her brother's subsequent interests and associations with Mexican theater. Finally, his extensive work as a scriptwriter for Mexican cinema undoubtedly fueled a desire to test his artistic abilities in the theater. It is not surprising, then, that he immersed himself in theatrical activities, beginning in 1946 with the La Linterna Mágica group, which was under the direction of Ignacio Retes. Through his friendship with Retes, Revueltas offered his services in

134

various capacities to La Linterna Mágica, which was subsidized by the Mexican Electricians Union.[3] During the group's second season, in 1947, Revueltas functioned as a guest director, staging Alexander Pushkin's one-act play <u>Mozart and Salieri</u>. In the following year, La Linterna Mágica proudly announced the staging of Revueltas's <u>Israel</u>, the first work written by a member of the group.

Israel (1947)

Revueltas's first play debuted on 13 May 1948 in a small theater rented and operated by the Mexican Electricians Union. It was directed by Ignacio Retes, who also acted the role of a secondary character. The script was published in the same year and was dedicated to Retes and the Linterna Mágica group.[4] Music by Silvestre Revueltas and a poem by Langston Hughes were included in the stage presentation. Salvador Novo recalled the opening night of <u>Israel</u> and how, as usual, "all the 'Intelligentsia' was present."[5] If artists and intellectuals displayed great interest in <u>Israel</u>, however, the general public did not. Few critics took note, and <u>Israel</u> was never to be produced again.

The setting for <u>Israel</u> is a small town in Texas, near the Mexican border. The characters are principally rural blacks, with the exception of a white Texas Ranger and a Mexican-American, who is the central character. The primary themes of racial prejudice and social alienation propel the limited action of this three-act play.

Act I occurs in the modest residence of Israel Smith, a black plumber. Israel's mother, Mama Smith, and his wife, Celeste, are waiting for Israel

to return home from work. In the meantime,
Rebeca, Israel's daughter, helps her mother and
grandmother prepare the house for a party which is
to celebrate the family's departure from Amapola
Village. The once-bucolic Texas town has changed
into a depressing center of bigotry and oppression
with the arrival of Standard Oil and the opening of
the oil fields. The Smiths hope to find a new life
in Florida. As the preparations for the party
continue, Mama Smith and Celeste learn of
Rebeca's love for Jimmy González, a young
Mexican-American. Rebeca's intention to marry
González shocks the two older women since they
consider the Mexican-American to be white.
Meanwhile, Esaú, Rebeca's older brother, arrives
home and announces that he has seen Israel in a
tavern. When Esaú admires a pair of his sister's
nylon stockings, he discovers that they were a gift
from Peggy Ryan, a white prostitute in their town.
He further discovers that his father, Israel, had
been in Ryan's house working that very day. At
this point, Uncle Eleazar, a mute, appears at the
house drunk, mysteriously carrying Israel's plumbing
wrench, which is covered with blood. Fearing that
Eleazar may have killed Israel, the family watches
as the mute coaxes Celeste outside of the house.
Esaú quickly leaves to dispose of the wrench.
Meanwhile, Jhonaton (sic) Fletcher, a young black
man, arrives.[6] Fletcher had been engaged to a girl
who was gang-raped by a group of white men.
Esaú returns to the house and announces that he
has found Jimmy González lurking in the shadows
nearby. Celeste then returns and informs them
that Peggy Ryan's dead body is outside. As if in
harmony, all thoughts and actions anticipate the
imminent danger--false accusations and
mistreatment at the hands of the white community.

In a desperate panic, everyone except Rebeca decides to flee. She remains behind to wait for Jimmy González.

Act II shifts to the local county jail, where Uncle Eleazar, Fletcher, and Jimmy González share a cell. Israel, who never actually appears on stage, is presumably isolated in another cell. All four men have been arrested and charged with the murder of Peggy Ryan. The action centers on a dialogue between Fletcher and González, the former being highly suspicious and resentful of the Mexican-American. In an initial effort to ignore González's entreaties to friendship, Fletcher pretends to have a conversation with Uncle Eleazar, the mute. To do so, Fletcher takes both parts in the dialogue. Slowly, however, González wins Fletcher's trust. The tension heightens when a Texas Ranger arrives to interrogate Eleazar by beating him. In the meantime, González proposes a plan for escape. Act II ends with Fletcher befriending González.

Act III takes place inside a petroleum pipeline that is scheduled to be opened and flooded with oil in a matter of hours. The Smith family, in accordance with González's plan, is to rendezvous with Israel and the others at a specified point in the pipeline. From there they are to cross, underground, into Mexico. Through miscalculations, however, they are trapped in the pipeline. They hear a voice they believe to be that of Israel, but it is Eleazar, who has miraculously been given Israel's voice, upon the death of the latter. Through Eleazar they learn that Fletcher and González were also killed, and that it was the local sheriff who had planted Ryan's body near their house. The play ends as the Smith family, trapped in the pipeline, awaits certain death.

John B. Nomland has suggested that Israel was inspired by Jean-Paul Sartre's 1946 play, La Putain respectueuse (The Respectful Prostitute).7 That Revueltas knew Sartre's work is highly probable, since it was staged in Mexico City in November 1947 by the Modern Art Theater. Three factors appear to indicate a connection between Israel and the French play. First, the emergence of Sartre as an international giant in drama undoubtedly attracted Revueltas's attention as the latter initiated himself in the theater. Second, both plays are clear attempts to describe and analyze racial discrimination in the southern United States. Finally, Revueltas's play exhibits, in general terms, an existentialist orientation not unlike that of Sartre during the same period.

In spite of important similarities, however, between Israel and La Putain respectueuse, significant differences exist. Revueltas's play is highly original and owes no parentage to Sartre for its plot and characters. On the contrary, Israel was a natural outgrowth of Revueltas's political and social world view. The author's treatment of class conflict and the moral corruption of capitalism (with a distinctly anti-American tone) are very much present in Israel. In short, Revueltas indicts an American society that is based on bigotry and exploitation.

The author's attempt to depict the culture of American blacks, although laudable, is somewhat lacking. Revueltas himself admitted in later years that Israel was an unsuccessful portrait of black Americans.8 Nevertheless, at least one critic reacted favorably in 1948, believing naively that the psychology of Texas blacks had been accurately captured by such items as colorful dress, a desire to dance, and a general ingenuousness.9 These elements, unfortunately, result in little more than caricature. In fact, it can be argued that all characters in Israel are pathetic stereotypes which serve to distort the very reality under examination.

Equally impoverished is the propagandistic treatment of white society, symbolized by the only white character, a Texas Ranger whose few lines are spoken in English with Spanish syntax. Commenting in a review of Israel, Thelma Ortiz stated: "The latter (the Ranger), a character too grossly exaggerated to be convincing, will be laughable to readers familiar with English because of the startling medley of his speech--English spoken in Spanish word order."[10] The Ranger, a totally brutal and vulgar character, is limited to a brief appearance in which he inflicts torture. Through the dialogues of the other characters, however, we learn of other whites: Peggy Ryan, the prostitute; Sheriff Stephenson, who illegally imprisons blacks; and a gang of unknown whites who raped Fletcher's girl friend. Not surprisingly there is mention of the Ku Klux Klan. Mama Smith indicts Standard Oil for having destroyed the tranquility of Amapola Village.

While the blacks are uniformly presented as kindly victims of persecution, and the whites are vicious bigots, one character, Jimmy González, represents a transcendent role. González is clearly the intended hero, full of compassion and understanding. He offers hope not only for Rebeca but for her whole family by tantalizing them with visions of the "promised land," Mexico. All of this becomes a bit ridiculous, though, when cast against Revueltas's lifelong attempt to expose the inequities and base corruption of Mexican society. Revueltas's view of his own country and countrymen does not square with González's assertion that in Mexico "blacks and whites are brothers."[11]

There are defects other than the characters to be noted in Israel. Structurally the play is poorly balanced. While the first act includes adequate action and plot development, the last two acts unfortunately fail in most respects. Noticeable are the many lengthy parts in which characters issue long and involved philosophical pronouncements. One reviewer has observed that the entire play "derails in the discursive second and third acts."[12] Also disturbing is the heavy emphasis upon biblical language, which, while congruent with the deeply fundamentalist mentality of many Texas blacks, is not convincing as everyday speech. Furthermore, it suggests an incoherent and unintentional symbolism which serves to confuse rather than elucidate the theme.

If Israel can be seriously faulted for its characters, structure, and language, it must be taken as a sincere attempt by Revueltas to transfer his considerable artistic talents to the stage. Although Israel met with little success, Revueltas was not deterred, for two years later he wrote one of the most successful plays in the history of Mexican theater.

Quadrant of Solitude (1950)

El cuadrante de la soledad (Quadrant of Solitude) made its debut on 12 May 1950 in the Arbeu Theater in Mexico City.[13] The work was staged by the Mexican Theatrical Company (La Compañía Mexicana de Comedia) under the direction of Ignacio Retes. Unlike Israel, which played to a small, select audience in a non-commercial theater, Quadrant of Solitude was performed in a thoroughly professional setting, along with the attendant publicity. The play's promoters made much of Diego Rivera's participation as the set designer. The highly competent cast included both Rosaura Revueltas and Silvia Pinal. Quadrant, then, was a significant step for José Revueltas in that it was his first full-fledged entrance into legitimate Mexican theater. Unfortunately, it was also to be his last.

Whereas Israel had gone virtually unnoticed, Quadrant soon established a considerable reputation, both good and bad. It was the first play by a Mexican author ever to reach one hundred consecutive performances. Drama critics devoted many columns to the work. While some commentaries were favorable, others were not, especially those of leftist critics who opposed the play on ideological grounds. In any event, Quadrant must be viewed as Revueltas's high point in Mexican theater. In spite of its box-office success, however, the play was not published until 1971.[14]

The play's title, which is symbolic in several respects, is the name of a street in a seedy section of Mexico City. The play's setting calls for multiple staging, so that the spectator is privy to the interiors of various buildings on Solitude Street. In plain view are the lobby, two guest rooms, and a gymnasium in the Hotel Solitude. Facing the hotel, but also in view of the audience, is the Shanghai Café, consisting of a serving area and backroom. A large church serves as the backdrop. While the script calls for significant action in the street in front of the buildings, most of the play's crucial scenes are located in one of the various interiors. In 1950, such a theatrical

set was complicated and somewhat experimental,
calling for expert technical lighting as the scenes
shift quickly from one room to another.

Revueltas designated the time frame of his play
as "current." Since there is no reference to
historical personages or events, the work, in fact,
has maintained a surprising tone of modernity. The
problems of strikes, drugs, prostitution, and
criminal activity are as relevant today (if not more
so) as they were in 1950. What has changed,
however, is the public's awareness and sensitivity.
As Frank Dauster has observed, Quadrant was
"quite a shocker in its day, with sordid theme and
multiple stage setting, but twenty years later it is
obvious and melodramatic."15

A plot synopsis of Quadrant is rendered difficult
by the sheer complexity of interwoven relationships
between the characters. The principal story line
relates a complicated conspiracy involving drugs,
assassinations, a labor strike, and peripheral love
affairs. So intricate are the various intrigues that
it is doubtful that the average spectator could
grasp all of the relationships, real and imaginary,
in one viewing of the play. For the most part,
characters bond together in couples or pairs
(godfather-goddaughter, employer-employee, drug
pusher-addict, lovers, to name only a few), each
couple existing independently of the others. At the
same time, however, at least one member of each
pair is inextricably involved with another couple.
The various associations often border on the
improbable and, indeed, share certain similarities
with the American soap opera.

Central to the play's plot is Rupert, a hotel
desk clerk who works for his girl friend, Malena,
the owner of the Hotel Solitude. Rupert is a
seedy character who has many connections with the

criminal underground and the local police; he dabbles in illegal drugs, operates as a police informant, and offers his services as a paid assassin. As the play's action unfolds, it becomes apparent that Rupert is involved in an incredible web of double and triple crosses. Among other things, he has been assigned by the police to kill an old friend from his criminal past, Caimán López. The latter, unbeknownst to Rupert, also works for the police and has successfully infiltrated the Central Committee of the Transportation Workers. Rupert also has promised to blow up a gasoline depository for the purpose of casting blame on the striking workers, and thus end the strike through government intervention. To accomplish this last goal, he convinces his "other" girl friend, Márgara, to coerce a local boxer, Kid Pancho, to do the dirty deed. Unfortunately for Rupert, Márgara manages to convince Kid Pancho to destroy the gasoline storage tanks by promising to run away with him. At the same time, Rupert has informed the striking workers that Kid Pancho intends to entrap them in the police plot. Rupert, of course, hopes that Kid Pancho will be discovered and killed by the strikers. Rupert's plan goes awry when it is discovered by Caimán López. The latter informs Kid Pancho that Rupert is working for the police. López further reveals that Rupert has incriminated Kid Pancho. When neither Rupert nor Kid Pancho blows up the petroleum storage facility, Malena, who loves Rupert, takes the task upon herself in order to save Rupert from the police. The entire episode is resolved when the body of Eduardo, a young student completely unconnected with the police plot, is discovered. Although his death is an apparent suicide, the police move quickly to take optimum advantage of

Eduardo's demise by preparing a report that will implicate him as the one responsible for bombing the gasoline depository. In this way, all of the various parties involved in the police plot are saved.

Although Rupert's complicated machinations form the pretext for the play, most of the action scenes deal with subplots involving a large number of secondary characters. Malena, for instance, has several lengthy conversations with Colombina, an aging prostitute who is sympathetically cared for by the hotel owner. One of the stranger couples populating Solitude Street is that of El Parches and his mysterious goddaughter, Piedad. The former is an organ grinder who wanders through the streets selling illegal drugs. Piedad is noteworthy for her ability to compose surreal poems on demand. Of tragic dimension is Kity, a young waitress at the Shanghai Café. A hardened drug addict, she is encouraged in her habit by her boss, Alfonso.

Another desperate couple is the young schoolteacher Enrique, and his nineteen-year-old student, Alicia. Their illicit love affair has recently escaped discovery by the timely intervention of another student, Eduardo, who falsely admits to having seduced Alicia in an effort to save Enrique from professional disaster. Eduardo, coincidentally, is in love with Kity. Motivated by his love, Eduardo attempts to extort money from Alicia's father, Evaristo, by promising him that he will leave town so as not to embarrass Alicia further. In reality, Eduardo intends the money to be used for Kity's drug rehabilitation.

The play reaches its climax when Evaristo and his friend Próspero make their way to Solitude Street to deliver the extortion money to Kity. Somewhat bewildered by the bizarre people they observe in the neighborhood (including an encounter with the prostitute Colombina), the two men are on the verge of accomplishing their mission when Eduardo's body is accidentally discovered in the restroom of the gymnasium, whereupon many of the play's loose ends are promptly resolved.

Each action encounter between members of the various couples in Quadrant reveals the intimate knowledge that Revueltas possessed of Mexico City's people and culture, particularly those of the lower classes. The characters are primarily representative of the criminal and socially marginal segments of society. The many compartmentalized encounters between characters, while failing to congeal into a larger, more conventional plot line, serve to reveal Mexican society and its problems through an open and candid interior view. The multiple stage setting permits numerous points of view, all of which pessimistically decry mental and physical degradation as a way of life. Colombina, for instance, reflects in matter-of-fact terms upon the life of a prostitute, commenting fully on its pains and supposed rewards. The illegal drug activities of Rupert, El Parches, and Alfonso are chillingly crass and carefree. Enrique's love affair with Alicia signals a breakdown of traditional values. Even Evaristo and Próspero, although seemingly benign, are judged guilty--the former because of his prior dealings with Colombina and the latter because of his illicit affair with Evaristo's wife. Perhaps the most disturbing characterization is that of Rupert. His totally amoral approach to life, which includes his nefarious alliance with the local police, serves as a pivotal point for the entire play. Finally, Eduardo, who by standard criteria must be judged the hero of Quadrant, commits suicide and thereby emphasizes the absolute absence of hope.

As if to prepare the audience, the spectator's program for performances of Quadrant, as well as the published script, included a personal announcement by Revueltas in which he stated that "Quadrant of Solitude does not seek applause."16 Rather, Revueltas insisted that the work had been written "to perturb and upset others as much as he is—naked and defenseless, ready to fight."17 He further observed that if art fulfilled its purpose, then the citizen would confront society's leaders and demand an accounting for what they have done to man. In short, Revueltas knew that his candid and explicit treatment of sex and drugs would shock the theatergoers of Mexico City. The emotional impact of Quadrant, however, was not meant to be sensationalist, but assaultingly jarring to the audience's social conscience.

In spite of Revueltas's stated goals, Quadrant's commercial success was based primarily on its thematic treatment of Mexico's social ills that were seldom openly discussed. But literary critics were concerned with other issues, namely numerous defects associated with the play's structure and character development. Miguel Guardia, for example, faulted Quadrant for its "confusion of relationships between the characters."18 Guardia also criticized the lack of resolution in the play's climax. Magaña Esquivel perceived problems with the play's structure: "Quadrant of Solitude is not, strictly speaking, a work of drama in that it does not sustain either an architecture or a method specific to this literary genre."19 Virtually all critics commented negatively on Diego Rivera's stage set.

The most caustic and vociferous criticisms came

from leftist critics, primarily political friends of Revueltas, who opposed the play on ideological and philosophical grounds. The attacks, in large part unwarranted, were similar to those mounted against Earthly Days (see Chapter 2). Quadrant was loudly censured for its obvious Sartrean influence. The leftist critics, in mimicking their French counterparts, denounced Revueltas for having sold out to the enemies of both man and the promise for a new tomorrow. Rafael Solana was moved to proclaim: "Revueltas is, in Mexico, the supreme pontiff of the school of scandals that in France has as its maximum exponent Sartre."[20]

Perhaps the most bitter and important criticism leveled against Quadrant was made by Juan Almagre (pseudonym for Antonio Rodríguez), who suggested, among other things, a dubious connection between Quadrant of Solitude and Sartre's Morts sans sépulture. Almagre contended that both Revueltas and Sartre were "the product of the same social decomposition; the same poverty of spirit; the same lack of faith in man."[21] Almagre's attack reached a frenzy when he asserted that Revueltas was "lost, definitively, as a revolutionary and a man."[22]

Revueltas was clearly moved and disturbed by the fervor of attacks upon his political integrity. Three days after Almagre's attack in El Nacional, Revueltas published a defense and counterattack in the newspaper in which he categorically denied all of Almagre's accusations.[23] Furthermore, Revueltas earnestly reaffirmed his loyalty and trust in the international Communist movement. At the same time, he accused Almagre for having "proceeded with extreme violence, injustice, and rancor."[24] Almagre was not impressed with

Revueltas's cries of innocence, however, for he responded three days later with yet another attack. His reply to Revueltas was pointed and uncompromising. Among the many charges he leveled was that Revueltas had fallen prey to a "false and impure aesthetic movement . . . that only sees moral misery and corruption in man."[25] Almagre went on to observe that despite Revueltas's assertions to the contrary, the writer would be judged by his works and not by his newspaper letters. On this point Almagre specifically cited The Stone Knife, Earthly Days, and Quadrant of Solitude as works illustrative of a "negative and destructive writer."[26] Perhaps most damaging was Almagre's suggestion that Revueltas had misrepresented the proletariat by characterizing it at its worst.

On the same day that Almagre responded to Revueltas, Ramírez y Ramírez initiated his three-part series condemning Earthly Days for its political and existentialist content (see Chapter 2).[27] Apparently the combined effect of the criticism made by both Almagre and Ramírez had an immediate impact on Revueltas, for on 16 June he published a public denunciation of his own literary works.[28] Revueltas requested that the publishers of Earthly Days immediately cease sales of the work. In addition, he stated: "I have also decided to ask the company that brought Quadrant of Solitude to the stage to suspend the performances of that work."[29] Revueltas charged himself with being guilty of presenting a false human and social reality in Quadrant.

Thus the great ideological and literary polemics that surrounded the publication of Earthly Days were brought to a climax with the debate over Quadrant of Solitude. The result was a total and definitive recanting by Revueltas in the face of his critics. Quadrant of Solitude, Revueltas's best and most successful play, was disavowed by its author and it faded into the history of Mexican theater. Revueltas had experienced the same intimidation that so many other Marxist writers in Europe and Latin America had undergone. Accused of having abandoned a political credo to which he fervently subscribed, the writer had little choice but to denounce his own literary work.

Pito Pérez in a Fix

Pito Pérez en la hoguera (Pito Pérez in a Fix) was written in the mid-1950s. Although its exact date is unknown, Revueltas once recalled, with some uncertainty, having written the work in 1955.[30] While the play was never published, it was performed late in Revueltas's life with his limited collaboration. Pito Pérez debuted in the Teatro Orientación in Mexico City on 7 August 1975. Its performances were limited in number and went unnoticed by critics.

Two things make Pito Pérez in a Fix unique in Revueltas's literature. First, it represents the only time Revueltas borrowed another author's fictional character. The figure of Pito Pérez, made famous by José Rubén Romero in his picaresque novel La vida inútil de Pito Pérez, was appropriated as Revueltas's protagonist. Romero was given credit in the script with the notation that the play was a "farce inspired by the popular character of the same name, in a free version."[31] The other unique factor found in the play is the highly developed comedy. Although Revueltas possessed a broad and rich sense of humor, he seldom employed it for

literary purposes. In <u>Pito Pérez</u>, however, the
spectator is treated to a wide arsenal of comic
devices   congruent   with   the   picaresque
tradition--irony, black humor, slapstick, and
wordplay. By adopting an established <u>pícaro</u> as his
central character, Revueltas was invited to give
full vent to his humorous vein.

There are considerable parallels between
Revueltas's Pito and Romero's. Both are drunks
and fugitives from justice. They are highly
intelligent, living by their wits on the margins of
society. While both possess rather loose codes of
personal conduct and ethics, they are also loveable.
Revueltas used Romero's pretext for Pito's life
story whereby the <u>pícaro</u> is urged by a poet to
relate his life in exchange for a bottle of wine.
Unlike Romero, however, who has his protagonist
relate a series of adventures, Revueltas structured
his play around a single episode.

<u>Pito Pérez in a Fix</u> begins with a prologue in
which the poet encounters a very drunk Pito in a
church belfry. After some cajoling, Pito agrees to
narrate the first significant event in his life. The
stage lights quickly dim and Act I commences.
The setting is a faintly lighted area near the ruins
of an abandoned convent. Pito, disguised as a
Franciscan friar to avoid capture by the police,
chances upon Camila Sánchez, who is praying to
God for a sign of hope in her struggle against the
government's tyranny. Camila mistakenly takes
Pito to be a vision, until the outrageous <u>pícaro</u>
manages to kiss and fondle her. But when his
advances go too far she concludes that he is a
fake, until she sees his Franciscan habit. She then
mistakes him for Father Serafín, who is being sent
to the region to direct the local struggle against
the government's attempt to ban religion in the

schools. The opportunistic Pito takes advantage of the mistaken identity and leaves with Camila for the nearby town.

Act II occurs in the local church's rectory, where Pito, still asleep, has spent the night in the same bedroom with Camila. With sublime naiveté, she tells the rectory maid how Pito, suffering from somnambulism, had gone to her bed and, thinking she was a wounded deer, had caressed her body to comfort her. Meanwhile, Torcuato, the maid's husband, arrives with packages of political propaganda. It is revealed that Camila is the president of the local "Redemption League," which uses the rectory as a base of operations against the "Tyrant," an anonymous government figurehead who is leading a relentless battle against the church. Suddenly Pito awakens and, having forgotten about his masquerade, believes himself to be at an inn. He recalls the circumstances under which he arrived at the rectory and quickly regains his composure just in time for the visit of the Comisario, a local government leader. The Comisario has come to demand that a wanted poster citing Pito Pérez as a fugitive be displayed on the church walls. Pito, feigning great surprise, convinces Camila that the wanted man is his twin brother and is innocent of all charges other than "social disillusionment."[32] The naive Camila believes him and promises to hide and protect the fugitive should he pass by the area.

As Camila learns more about the fictitious twin brother, her curiosity grows to such a point that she wants to meet him. The real Pito tells her that he is in the house at that very minute, sleeping in an adjoining bedroom. But Pito's farce takes on proportions of reality when a voice speaks to them from behind the bedroom door. When

Camila is called away, the bewildered Pito demands to know, without success, who is speaking to him. The mysterious voice tells him to be patient and orders him to listen for a whistle. One blow indicates that he is to cease talking; two blows signify that he is to begin talking immediately.

The play climaxes with the arrival of a local factory owner named Don Justo, the Comisario, Camila, and three elected officials from the town council. They have come to announce a new alliance between the church and the government. Camila views the alliance as treason and turns to Pito for support, but the hapless pícaro is controlled in his conversation by the whistle behind the door. It is decided that the "Tyrant" will be replaced by a new leader, selected by lottery from those present in the room. The Comisario warns that whoever is elected must keep it a secret, because the strength of the tyranny is its anonymity. All agree, and they draw lots from a hat.

Meanwhile, an angry crowd demanding justice arrives, along with the real Father Serafín, who identifies Pito and demands his arrest. Camila intercedes to save Pito, but in the process realizes that he has deceived her. Pito quickly admits his identity and guilt, but informs them that he is the new "Tyrant" as a result of the lottery. Screaming for justice, the crowd outside demands that the "Tyrant" be burned. Pito is then thrown into the street to meet his just reward. The play ends with the discovery that the mysterious voice in the bedroom had been that of Father Pinillos, the local parish priest.

Although the play's protagonist was borrowed from Romero's classic novel, Pito Pérez in a Fix is highly original and carries its author's unique political stamp. Also in evidence is an autobiographical undercurrent that surfaces in the presentation and characterization of the pícaro. This aspect reveals a curious self-criticism on the part of Revueltas that is both extremely penetrating and humorous. Pito's discursive ramblings often point to events and observations that suggest an ironic self-portrait of Revueltas. Indeed, Malkah Rabell has referred to the play as a kind of "autoburla."33 There are numerous parallels between Revueltas's life and that of the luckless Pito Pérez. In an interview shortly after the play's debut, Ignacio Hernández followed this line of inquiry with Revueltas. The latter, somewhat coyly, agreed that several items were more than coincidence.34 The most interesting parallel concerns the various criminal charges for which Pito is sought by the police. They are, in large part, the same charges leveled against the author in 1968 as the result of the student riots. If this latter similarity was intended, it points to revision of the original script, since the play was first written in 1955, long before the author's involvement with the Student Movement.

In any event, it is highly probable that the play's greatest significance resides precisely in the fact that it affords an interior view of Revueltas seldom seen by the literary public. The author's penchant for hopeless causes, his ability to maintain a good-natured idealism in the face of persecution, and his boundless selflessness are all present in his personalized rendition of the roguish Pito. Commenting on his fugitive status, the pícaro (Revueltas) observes that he is considered a reprobate by those who are "poor in spirit, hypocrites, Pharisees."35 Even more revealing is the introspective notation that Pito (the author) "represents the tormented conscience that rises up, inert and solitary, in the face of the powerful, the prevaricators, and those who dispense with morals and principles."36 Although the analysis sounds self-serving, it is not. Revueltas probably felt comfortable in inserting such praiseworthy qualities because Pito is, in the final view, a rogue. As Revueltas states: "My brother Pito Pérez is a crazy man, a poor devil and nothing more!"37

When considered for its literary qualities, Pito Pérez in a Fix is not without value. Above all, Revueltas's humorous treatment of Mexican politics during the War of the Christers is entertaining. Interestingly enough, the author displays sympathy toward the church's cause when confronting the government's tyranny. The play may be faulted, however, for structural defects and a lack of resolution. There is considerable imbalance between the two acts; the first operates essentially as a pretext for the rest of the work. The political and social relationships among the various characters are ill-defined, and they send the spectator seeking answers to questions that were most likely intended to be readily answered in the play's context.

They'll Be Waiting for Us In Abril (1956)

Although Nos esperan en Abril (They'll Be Waiting for Us In Abril) was neither produced nor published, for years it was circulated among the author's friends and other writers. José Agustín, for example, makes mention of the play in his "Epilogue" for Revueltas's Obra literaria.38 Sometime in 1956, the work made its way to

Europe by means of the author's sister, Rosaura.
A translation of the play was apparently presented
to Bertold Brecht, who, according to Revueltas,
was preparing rehearsals for its production at the
time of his death.[39] The original manuscript
carries a dedication to Rosaura Revueltas and is
dated 1956, which, if correct, makes They'll Be
Waiting for Us in Abril Revueltas's last play,
having been written shortly after Pito Pérez in a
Fix.

Abril is probably Revueltas's best play. That it
was never produced in Mexico is undoubtedly due
to its political content. In an interview with
Ignacio Hernández, Revueltas claimed that he saw
little possibility of staging Abril because "it is a
work that demands a level of political
sophistication not present in the Mexican public."[40]
Indeed, Abril is one of Revueltas's most involved
and intricate works from a political standpoint. He
undertakes an exhaustive investigation of such
complex issues as Party loyalty, freedom of the
individual, and historical consciousness. Above all,
it treats the very personal question of expulsion for
unpardonable "errors" from the Communist party
during the Stalinist period. It is significant to note
that Revueltas wrote Abril during the very time
that he was anxiously seeking readmittance to the
Mexican Communist party, after being persona non
grata for some six years. It follows, therefore,
that Abril was conceived as an example of Marxist
literature to promote his candidacy for reentry into
the Party.

Many of the political discussions present in
Abril are sympathetic to the Party's need and right
to punish and correct a member's "errors." Party
leadership is generally portrayed in favorable terms.
These elements, as well as others, have prompted

José Agustín to assess Abril as one of Revueltas's
"more conventional Marxist works," comparing it to
The Motives of Cain.[41]   Agustín's observation does
not seem entirely justified, however, since there
are numerous circumstances in Abril that suggest
an insensitivity on the part of the Communist party
toward its most devoted workers.   Furthermore, a
host of factors such as the Communist hero's
suicidal decision to die in the hands of his enemies
rather than carry on the fight for socialism,
suggests a less than conventional Marxist work.   In
short, Abril is a balanced examination of the
Communist party that neither denounces nor
vindicates Party politics.   It may well be that
Revueltas, upon completing the play, was unsure
about its probable impact.

Abril is set in the fictitious countries of
Aquitania and Anatolia.   Specific references to the
Spanish Civil War and the presence of the Red
Army suggest a European environment.   The time
line, 1938 to 1945, underscores a clear intent to
focus the political themes within the context of
global history during the Second World War.   At
work are the forces of fascism, communism, and
democratic socialism.

Act I takes place in a prison cell in Ciudad
María, capital of Aquitania.   Present is Marcos
Ríos, the local leader of the Communist party, who
has been sentenced to die for his role in an
abortive rebellion five months earlier.   The action
is limited to conversations between Marcos and
various persons who visit him on the eve of his
scheduled execution.   The discussions disclose a
complex political situation surrounding Marcos's
imprisonment.   Through his encounter with the
prison warden, it is learned that the Social
Democrats, who control the government, have been

pressured by the Fascists into executing Marcos.
He is then visited by a chaplain who cryptically
tells Marcos to look for special signs that will
indicate his imminent escape from prison.

The chaplain's departure is followed by the
arrival of Renata, Marcos's wife, who explains that
the chaplain is, in fact, a Party worker and that
the Communists are planning Marcos's escape that
very evening. The Party wants Marcos alive so
they can expel him for leading an armed revolt
against the better judgment of the Party's
leadership. Renata tries to persuade her husband
to avoid the disgrace of expulsion by remaining in
prison and being executed. Undoubtedly mirroring
Revueltas's thoughts on the matter in 1956, Renata
exclaims that "I want to save you from the darkest
and most terrible destiny that can await a
Communist--to end his days as an enemy of the
Party."42 To Marcos's surprise, Renata confesses
that she never believed in his uprising and that if
he lives, she too will have to vote for his
expulsion. Act I ends with a visit from Deputy
Franchi, a major figure in the Social Democrats'
government. Franchi informs Marcos that the
prison officials will do nothing to stop the
Communists' escape plans and, furthermore, that
Marcos will be commissioned to deliver a message
to his party indicating the Social Democrats' desire
to form a united front against the Fascists.

Act II transpires several days later in the
neighboring Republic of Anatolia. The scene is a
country house near the border. Present are
Renata, a Party worker named Claudio, and Bruno,
who has replaced Marcos Ríos as head of the
Communist party. An atmosphere of anxiety
prevails as they desperately try to communicate by
radio with their forces in Aquitania. Their primary

concern is whether Marcos has successfully escaped
from prison. Act II is essentially devoted to long
and complicated political discussions centering on
Party loyalty and Marcos Ríos. Bruno accuses Ríos
of errors that can neither be rectified nor
pardoned. He posits the notion of Marcos's
nonexistence in an historical sense. The discussions
end, however, when a newspaper arrives announcing
Marcos's death subsequent to his escape. Everyone
is stunned when Marcos suddenly appears at the
house. The newspaper accounts had been falsified
to facilitate his crossing the border.

Act III returns to Aquitania six years later; the
scene is the headquarters of the Communist party.
A long conversation between Claudio and Renata
reveals several important developments. Ríos had
been expelled from the Party in 1939; only his
closest friends know that he is alive and continues
to work for the Party under an alias. Since the
Communists are on the verge of taking power in
Aquitania with the help of the Red Army, Claudio
and Renata decide that the time is opportune to
request Marcos's readmission to the Party. All
hopes of his readmission are dashed, however, when
Bruno arrives and informs them that the Social
Democrats plan to call for an investigation into
Ríos's death. They hope to prove that the
Communists killed him.

A crisis concerning Marcos's future with the
Party emerges. He cannot reappear after six years
of silence without assuming his previous role as a
major Party figure, but this would be impossible
because he is not even a member. Bruno suggests
that Marcos write a declaration, thereby proving
that he was not killed. In addition, he must
definitively renounce his role in politics and the
Party. But Marcos refuses to cooperate. Two

Party workers arrive; one worker seeks permission to join a band of guerrillas recently formed in the town of Abril. When Marcos hears this, he too decides to join the group. When they learn that the Fascists are about to raid their headquarters, Renata proclaims her intention to join the guerrillas with Marcos. The latter suddenly changes his mind and decides to remain in the offices and be killed by the Fascists as a kind of personal testament. As the play ends, Renata bids Marcos farewell.

They'll Be Waiting for Us in Abril is perhaps most important as an explication of Revueltas's ethical and political concerns during the 1950s. The work displays a maturity and profundity not present in his other works of the same period. As a political commentary it deserves serious study, for it is much more than a propagandistic instrument designed to promote the Communists' cause. Rather, it is an honest and candid investigation of Party politics during the Stalinist period. Unfortunately, Abril requires a politically sophisticated audience. It is obvious, therefore, that the play is limited as a viable work of theater.

As a dramatic work, Abril demonstrates that Revueltas's abilities as a playwright had improved considerably since his first efforts. Unlike Israel and Quadrant of Solitude, Abril is structurally sound, possesses a coherent plot, and resolves itself by means of a clear and logical climax. The central characters are well developed and multi-dimensional. The most notable defect appears to be Revueltas's penchant for substituting vital dramatic dialogue with complicated discursive monologues. In any event, Abril was never tested for either its political or artistic viability. Rather,

it slipped into the author's files and still awaits
staging and publication.

The Dead Will Live (1947)

For many years it was believed that Revueltas
had written only four plays. Shortly after his
death in 1976, however, the photocopy of a fifth
play Los muertos vivirán (The Dead Will Live) was
discovered among the author's papers. A diligent
search failed to locate the original manuscript.
Unfortunately, the photocopy was of inferior quality
and resulted in the deletion of small, and
apparently nonsubstantive, fragments of dialogue.
Through careful and thoughtful study, these
fragments have been rewritten by Andrea Revueltas
and her husband, Philippe Chéron.[43]
The Dead was written during July and August
1947. Thus, properly speaking, it was Revueltas's
second play, following closely after Israel, which
was completed in May of the same year. The
author's personal correspondence during 1947
indicates that he intended the play for possible
staging with the Linterna Mágica group.[44]
Curiously, though, when Revueltas was once asked
to cite his plays, he made no mention of the
work.[45] He may have simply forgotten about it in
the intervening years, or perhaps he considered the
manuscript insufficiently polished to constitute a
finished work. Certainly the existing photocopied
version supports this latter possibility, since The
Dead is plagued with inconsistencies and an
illogical plot development. Whatever Revueltas's
reasons were for shelving the play, The Dead
disappeared for some thirty years.
The geographical setting for The Dead is

unspecified; it is only known that the locale is a major city in a country beset with political turmoil. A capsulized view of the play reveals a schematized treatment of the conflict between fascism and socialism. The central plot deals with a political conspiracy involving sabotage and an impending government coup d'état. The action begins at midnight on 23 December and terminates in the early morning of Christmas Day. The Socialist party, having learned that the Fascists have planned a take-over of the government on 25 December, contrives a scheme to blow up an electric plant a few hours prior to the intended coup. The loss of electrical power will presumably disrupt the Fascists' use of the radio as a means of controlling the populace. The Socialists' plan is to enter the plant and wire dynamite for detonation from outside the building the following day.

The setting for Act I is the home of Gregorio Medina, which is situated across the street from the electric plant. Medina, a young Socialist party worker, has been ordered to enter the plant secretly and install the dynamite. Another Socialist worker, Porfirio Galván, is assigned to detonate the explosives. The action begins with Porfirio, who is stationed near a window in Medina's living room, observing Medina successfully infiltrating the electric plant. Also present in the house is Elisa, Gregorio's wife, who is to flee the city with her children several hours prior to the detonation. Most of the action centers around a discussion between the two characters concerning the themes of life and death. Both Elisa and Porfirio grapple with the certainty that Gregorio will die during the explosions, since he is to remain in the plant until the detonation. Porfirio, after explaining to Elisa the plan for her escape from

the city, gives her a gun which as a last resort she
is to use on her children and herself should the
sabotage plan fail.

Act II shifts to the headquarters of the League
of Democracy, an ill-defined Fascist group that is
planning the coup d'état. In charge is Felipe
Dueñas, a onetime close friend of Medina. As the
final hour approaches, Dueñas is informed of the
Socialists' plot against the electric plant. In a
desperate effort to thwart it, Dueñas orders a
series of drastic measures, including a suicide squad
to enter the plant. There follows a dizzying series
of events. First a prisoner is captured by the
Fascists and taken to Dueñas's headquarters.
Unfortunately, the prisoner's face is mutilated
beyond recognition, thereby preventing
identification. Through the false testimony of
another Socialist prisoner, the Fascists are told
that the sole person responsible for the sabotaging
of the plant is Gregorio. The Fascists soon
become convinced that the unidentified prisoner is
Gregorio and that therefore the plan has been
successfully thwarted.

Act III returns to Medina's home, shortly before
the scheduled detonation. Elisa now realizes that
the sabotage plot has failed and prepares to kill
her two children and commit suicide in accordance
with the Party's instructions. Their deaths
surrender the house to the only remaining occupant,
Nana Casilda, a wetnurse. Socialist workers then
arrive at the house and, mistaking Nana for a
Fascist agent, kill her. When they find the family
dead, they read a love letter from Gregorio to
Elisa, telling her that he is alive and safe from all
danger, thanks to the intervention of Porfirio.

The discovery of The Dead Will Live is not
likely to enhance Revueltas's lackluster reputation

as a dramatist. The play's many inconsistencies and incoherent plot render it nearly incomprehensible at times. The end of Act II, for instance, witnesses the Fascists' celebrating their political victory, but Act III promptly discloses that, in fact, the Socialists are in control of the government. In any event, until a determination can be made concerning the definitiveness of the existing version of <u>The Dead</u>, any appraisal would be tentative at best.

Chapter Five

The Essays

José Revueltas's production as an essayist was prodigious. Indeed, the sheer volume of his collected essays would rival that of his fiction. Unfortunately, because of space limitations, only a portion of his essays can be discussed here. Many of the author's most important essays were not published during his lifetime. Those that were published, more often than not, appeared in marginal journals of modest circulation or in limited editions prepared by small publishing houses. Even today, although many of his essays have been published posthumously, a large number have yet to appear.[1]

Revueltas's essays assumed many forms: newspaper articles, letters, memoranda, political announcements, printed lectures, monographs, and book-length studies. The literary style employed in these works ranges widely, from simple, clear discourse designed for mass popular consumption to complex, technical treatments of formal philosophic problems. Throughout most of the essays there is a powerful argumentative current that reveals the passion and sincerity with which Revueltas presented his philosophical views, most notably those associated with his independent Marxism. While the essays often require great effort on the part of the reader, there is a rich analytical world-view to uncover, for those willing to do so.

For various political and economic reasons, Revueltas often experienced difficulties in securing publishers for his literature, especially for his essays. In spite of the fact that for years many of his essays remained in relative obscurity, it is clear that Revueltas assigned great significance to them. When Revueltas died in 1976, his friend Rodolfo Rojas Zea observed that Revueltas "considered his philosophic works, which are almost unknown, to be his most important."[2] This notion was reaffirmed by Andrea Revueltas and Philippe Chéron in their "Presentación" to Cuestionamientos e intenciones (Questions and Intentions). As they observe, Revueltas was extremely distraught over his failure to publish his essays because he considered them to be "the most important aspect of his literary production."[3]

Although Revueltas wrote essays from his earliest days as a writer, his most important works of nonfiction were produced in the later stages of his literary career. In general terms, as his activity in fiction steadily lessened throughout his life, his production of essays intensified. This was particularly true during the last five years of his life, when he feverishly wrote and edited numerous major essays while producing no fiction whatsoever. Taken as a whole, Revueltas's essays reveal the fascinating evolution of one of Latin America's most original thinkers. His works are not only important for their insightful content, but for the many helpful keys that they provide for a deeper understanding of his fiction. Even though Revueltas wrote on a wide variety of topics in his essays, the overwhelming majority of them treated two issues vital to his life: aesthetics and politics.

Aesthetics

Revueltas was extremely interested in all forms of art. He wrote on music, painting, theater, and film. It was literature, however, that most preoccupied him in his essays on aesthetics. In discussing Revueltas's concern with literary criticism and theory, Márgara Russotto has observed: "Seldom, in Latin American literature, has there been such an important symbiosis between creation and theoretical reflection as occurs in this author."[4] Revueltas's constant interest in the role of literature and the artist, literary style, ideology and literature, and the relationship between literature and the state remained with him throughout his life.

With the exception of a few essays, most of Revueltas's earliest nonfiction appeared in his newspaper column, "La marea de los días," in El Popular (see Chapter 1). Contemporaneous to that series he wrote additional essays for the same newspaper. One of the most interesting was "An Appraisal of Juan Ramón Jiménez: Somber America" (the essays' original Spanish titles appear in the notes), in which Revueltas forcefully attacked the Spanish poet for having criticized Pablo Neruda's poetry.[5] The article, which provoked a minor polemic, revealed a youthful and enthusiastic author in verbal battle with one of the titans of Spanish literature.

In the 1940s two other important literary essays appeared that illustrate Revueltas's early theoretical concerns with regard to Mexican literature. The first, "Response to the Novel: The Rattlesnake to the Cat," published in 1943, was an attempt to analyze the state of the Mexican novel.[6] Arguing persuasively that the Mexican novel was not revolutionary because most writers' fortunes were attached to the interests of the bourgeoisie, he called for the writers to study the nation's reality and to penetrate the meaning of the dialectic movement of history. The article's brevity, however, prevented a full exploration of the problems cited. In 1946 Revueltas elaborated his positions in "The Novel, Mexico's Task."[7] Revueltas argued that the Mexican novel was not in crisis and, in fact, had a bright future. In suggesting that true revolutionary art was based on realism, he advanced the concepts of critical realism and dialectical realism as fundamental to any investigation of Mexico's reality. He called on novelists to discard their prejudices and treat Mexico's people without regard to any specific political or ethical stance.

During the next several years Revueltas was preoccupied with politics and the Mexican Communist party. He was unexpectedly forced to return to the issue of art and literature in 1950, however, as a result of the polemics surrounding Earthly Days and Quadrant of Solitude. He wrote various documents at that time (already discussed in Chapters 2 and 4). In addition, he wrote an extensive treatise on Socialist Realism, "Concerning the Questions of Dialectical Materialism and Aesthetics with Respect to Earthly Days" which has only recently been published.[8] This position paper, which was not originally intended for publication, was sent personally to Vicente Lombardo Toledano and Enrique Ramírez. It is in this work that Revueltas fully displays, for the first time, his profound understanding of dialectical materialism and historical materialism with regard to art, and their relationship to Socialist Realism. Ironically, the careful and analytical presentation of his views on Socialist art were calculated to corroborate Ramírez's severe criticism of Earthly Days. While Revueltas's essay thoroughly discredited his own novel, it clearly demonstrated that he was a first-rate literary critic, especially from the Socialist point of view.

It was six years before Revueltas again turned to the essay as a means of defining and explaining his ideas on art and literature. In September 1956, only months after being readmitted to the Mexican Communist party, he completed Realism in Art, a study that treated the question of Socialist Realism.[9] Perhaps as an offering of good faith to Party officials, Revueltas's Realism in Art affirmed his loyalty and dedication to Socialist Realism, proclaiming it to be the only authentic approach for literature. He included an explanation of how the artist must capture the internal movement of reality through a conscientious evaluation, using the concepts of dialectical and historical materialism. He totally rejected the notion that Socialist Realism was "directed art." Revueltas insisted that Socialist writers produced works laudatory of socialism only because of their highly developed sense of duty. To write such works, writers employ, according to Revueltas, criticism and self-criticism to arrive at the truth. In spite of his rigorous defense of Socialist Realism, the Mexican author suggested that Communist writers in non-Communist countries must necessarily adopt methods and approaches not cultivated by their comrades in Socialist states. This observation, perhaps unwittingly, seemed to suggest that Mexican Communist writers should not be entirely bound by all the tenets of the old Socialist Realism of the past. In any event, Realism in Art was clearly an exposition on orthodox literary positions.

Although Revueltas would later reject the work's most basic tenets, the treatise must be viewed as a splendid example of literary theory in defense of a highly dubious partisan position.

In the spring of 1957 Revueltas visited Budapest. His arrival coincided with the immediate aftermath of the Hungarian uprisings of 1956. While in the capital city, Revueltas wrote "A Letter from Budapest to Communist Writers"10 in which he accused his fellow Communist writers of having fostered ideological deformations of reality in their literature. He asserted that these same writers had remained silent in the face of gross errors on the part of Stalin. Revueltas denounced the "cult of personality" and suggested that Socialist literature should have "truth" as its positive hero.

The accusations included in "Letter from Budapest" differed radically from the positions espoused in Realism in Art, even though the two works were written only months apart. Two fundamental reasons may be offered to explain Revueltas's apparently disparate positions. Realism in Art was undoubtedly contrived as a display of good faith to the Party and, hence, must be viewed with some suspicions concerning sincerity and intent. Once readmitted to the Mexican Communist party in 1956, Revueltas soon began an internal struggle within the Party to change or modify its policies and direction. "Letter from Budapest," although essentially a work dealing with aesthetics, was one of the first essays that promoted Revueltas's struggle for change. Yet another reason for the differences exhibited between the two works in question may be found in the dramatic changes that occurred during the post-Stalinist era, especially after the Twentieth

World Communist Congress in 1956, in which Khrushchev openly denounced Stalin and gave Communist writers new hope in their struggle for artistic freedom. By 1957, one year after it was written, Realism in Art was in many ways antiquated. Thus, while Realism in Art reflected a belated Stalinist orthodoxy, "Letter from Budapest" exemplified a post-Stalinist mentality.

Revueltas's essays from 1957 to 1963 were devoted primarily to political matters. Several works on literature were written during this period, however. In 1961, soon after being expelled from the Mexican Communist party, Revueltas wrote "Concerning Walls of Water," which was prepared for the 1961 edition of the novel (see Chapter 2).[11] This work is important because it is Revueltas's best explanation of what he called "dialectical realism," and how it is applied to literature. Yet another work dated 1961, but only recently published, is "Concerning a Revolutionary Connotation of Art."[12] Originally delivered as a lecture during the author's stay in Cuba, this exposition sought to establish an analogy between, on the one hand, man's relationship to nature with regards to modes of production, and on the other hand, the cultivation of a revolutionary (Socialist) literature. Revueltas argued that all art is necessarily historical and ideological. He further insisted that "rational" and productive art is based on realism, humanism, and dialectics.

A final example of Revueltas's essays during the period of time from 1957 to 1963 is "A Character by Gide and Some Ideas on Art."[13] It is here that Revueltas, for the first time, called for a higher notion of aesthetic consciousness, one that would transcend politics and social classes. While he conceded that "real art" would necessarily be "revolutionary and advanced," he totally rejected the orthodox belief that writers such as Sartre and Céline were politically of the "enemy" camp. "A Character by Gide" is a guidepost for most of Revueltas's subsequent writings on aesthetics in that it represented his definitive break with a purely Socialist point of view regarding art. He would progressively adopt a more ecumenical approach that nonetheless would never abandon the question of politics and class struggle as central issues in all art forms.

The greatest single flurry of essays on aesthetics occurred between 1965 and 1967. During this period Revueltas solidified and expanded upon his highly sophisticated theories of art. Perhaps the most notable work of this period is Theory and Problems of Film.[14] Relying on his many years of experience as a scriptwriter for Mexican cinema, Revueltas brought together in this essay a veritable feast of technical, practical, and theoretical concerns of film. The study begins with an attempt to place film within the arts. There is a fruitful discussion of cinematic use of poetical imagery and metaphor, cinema's relationship to literature and theater, and the film's structural components. Of particular interest is a penetrating comparison between film and the artistic qualities found in selected paintings by David Alfaro Siqueiros and José Clemente Orozco.

In the process of defining the differences between narrative and film, Revueltas introduced the reader to the craft of adapting a novel to cinema. To do this he selected a passage from Camus's La Femme adultère, and he proceeded to write an imaginative film script. Revueltas slowly dissected Camus's narrative for the reader and transformed its substance into the language of film.

The result is a kind of primer for would-be film adaptors. After treating a single scene from Camus's novel, Revueltas then turned to the larger question of film as a total work of art. He undertook a discussion of problems associated with integrating a film's various components. At its most basic level, a film's theme must first be determined. The theme is then expressed through dramatic construction whose movement is held together and propelled by montage. Not surprisingly, Revueltas concluded that montage is dialectical in nature.

Many other topics germane to cinematography are introduced in Theory and Problems of Film. There is, for example, an analysis of the differences between acting for stage and for film. Revueltas attempted to define the actor's artistic function in filmmaking. The investigation of this problem includes a rather complicated study of the actor's relationship to the film and its script. In his analysis Revueltas's fondness for dialectical subject-object dichotomies is present. Concluding his discussion, there is an explanation of the construction of a total script. Arguing that it is not a literary genre, Revueltas nonetheless established an elaborate system of dramatic categories for the film script. What is more, he based his system on an analysis of Dostoyevsky's Crime and Punishment.

After having examined the theory and problems of cinematography from numerous perspectives, Revueltas completed his study by applying his principles to two noteworthy cases. The first is an analysis of sex and alienation in Michelangelo Antonioni's L'Avventura. The second is a study of Charlie Chaplin's use of gestural language as communication in film. In both analyses, Revueltas displayed his considerable knowledge of film as art.

Perhaps as an afterthought, Revueltas included as appendixes to Theory and Problems of Film two essays on literature. One of these, "Literary Self-Analysis," was and is particularly significant.[15] In this work Revueltas first set forth his notion of literary self-analysis, a system whereby the writer can use his "materials" to capture the internal, objective "tendency" of the real. He was careful to distinguish his method of self-analysis from simple self-criticism. While the latter seeks to answer subjective and qualitative questions, self-analysis responds to an objective view of aesthetics. To achieve the necessary logic for his system, Revueltas argued, in Hegelian fashion, for the objective existence of an aesthetic content in the external world. A work of art is strictly governed not only by its internal-objective rules of organization, but may also be evaluated against a universal aesthetic order.

To illustrate his concept of "literary self-analysis," Revueltas analyzed various main characters in Errors (see Chapter 2). As a by-product of his central thesis, the author digressed in order to launch a frontal attack against Socialist Realism, which, Revueltas concluded, was antidialectical in nature. Although he conceded that socialism and communism would someday perfect human freedom, he insisted that this could be done only with the help of artists committed to truth.

One of Revueltas's best essays on art, "A Theoretical Schema for an Essay on the Questions of Art and Freedom," appeared in 1966.[16] In this work Revueltas revealed the profundity to which he had developed his ideas on aesthetics. Progressively relying on formal philosophical terminology and concepts, he sought to present art as an ideological superstructure. For Revueltas, art reflected the historical interests and contradictions of its time, but he argued that art is necessarily at odds with its immediate reality and is, in fact, a negation of it. The objects of both freedom and art are identical: man. Both freedom and art are inalienable and not subject to mediation by societies or governments. Thus, asserted Revueltas, both capitalism and socialism (neo–Stalinism) will fail in their attempt to control man's freedom and his art.

"A Soviet 'Freeze' on Free Expression of Thought" was also published in 1966.[17] It was an impassioned defense of two Soviet writers, Andrés Siniavsky (Abram Tertz) and Yuli Daniel. Both men were arrested, tried, and sentenced to hard labor in 1966 for supposedly publishing anti–Soviet literature outside the Soviet Union. In arguing, once again, that art must supersede the conflict between socialism and capitalism, Revueltas attacked the Soviet judicial system for its outrageous persecution of writers. In Revueltas's estimation, free expression had become a clandestine activity in the Soviet Union.

In 1967, the editors of Revueltas's Obra literaria invited him to write a prologue to his works. The result was a major statement on his own literature, "The Author's Prologue to the Present Edition."[18] This essay offers the reader an intimate view of Revueltas's thoughts concerning his efforts as an artist. He included a full explanation of the controversy surrounding Earthly Days, a commentary on freedom and art, a rather abstract discussion of consciousness and the writer, and a study of the relationship among the writer, the self, and the reader.

In the same year, Revueltas published "My Essential Position," yet another essay on art.[19] In the work he limited his observations to the "method" of the novel which, according to him, operates at two levels--its intrinsic direction and its structure. The latter, in turn, is divided into quantitative components (plot, action, and the circumstances of the characters) and qualitative components (the characters' situations). Echoing ideas of Sartre, Revueltas went on to discuss human contingency (both opaque and diaphanous) as it relates to the writing of novels. In addition, he included a discussion of man's anthropomorphism and the notion of "otherness."

As Revueltas's understanding of aesthetics became more sophisticated throughout the 1960s, he often produced highly abstract essays written in technical language. To explain his positions he began to rely on formal philosophical terminology, much of it taken from Marx, Hegel, Sartre, Lukács, and Althusser, to name but a few. More and more Revueltas began to support his ideas through open references to established authorities. At the same time, however, it is undeniable that Revueltas's ideas were original syntheses.

A good example of the abstract essay is "Problems of Aesthetic Knowledge," written in 1967.[20] The author first returned to the issue of an objective aesthetics, treated in earlier essays, but with a new twist. After reviewing Lukács's ideas on art, and finding general agreement with the great Socialist theoretician, Revueltas concluded that Lukács has insufficiently analyzed the question of an objective aesthetics. In addressing himself to the issue, Revueltas surprisingly concluded that since dialectical materialism and Marxism are based on the search for the dissolution of man's alienation, true art should speak to the most basically human aspect of man, that is, without respect to his social or historical contingency. In advancing this idea, Revueltas essentially denied the validity of all Socialist art of the period, for he suggested an artistic concept totally contrary to Socialist Realism. Ironically, Revueltas based his argument primarily on Marx's Economic and Philosophical Manuscripts of 1844 and a passage from Shakespeare's Romeo and Juliet.

"The Mexican School of Painting and the Novel of the Mexican Revolution," written and published in 1967, also deserves mention.[21] After leading the reader through a complicated historical and social analysis of Mexico's history, Revueltas argued that both Mexican painters and novelists had failed to capture the internal realities of the Mexican Revolution. He accused painters such as Diego Rivera of having distorted the ideology of the revolution through a puppetlike adherence to Socialist Realism. Concerning the novelists who produced the so-called Novel of the Mexican Revolution, Revueltas asserted that these writers had created a purely mythic image of the Revolution that served bourgeois purposes.

With his participation in the Student Movement of 1968, Revueltas abruptly turned his attention to the political essay and virtually abandoned aesthetics as a topic. In 1970, however, while still imprisoned in Lecumberri, he wrote a prologue for what was to be a collection of his essays on aesthetics.[22] Although Revueltas was never able to publish the book, volume 18 of his Obras Completas, Cuestionamientos e intenciones, is essentially the book that Revueltas had planned. His prologue is a highly abstract explanation of the historical and political forces in operation during the writing of his essays on aesthetics from 1963 to 1967.

After his release from Lecumberri in 1971, Revueltas published only a few additional essays on art and the artist.23 One work, "Literature and Liberation in Latin America," is particularly significant.24 As an attempt to fuse his political theory with the question of literature, this essay is one of Revueltas's most impressive. Central to the work's thesis is the notion that art is a form of organized consciousness and, as such, can promote the eradication of man's alienation and the liberation of Latin America. As the underdeveloped countries in Latin America seek to break away from North American domination and pursue their own nationalism, they must, Revueltas warned, do so within a context of internationalism. This is also true with respect to Latin American literature. Thus, he concluded, only writers such as Juan Carlos Onetti, Alejo Carpentier, and Ernesto Sábato are functional in promoting the liberation of Latin America because they universalize their national milieu. Conversely, writers such as Carlos Fuentes and Julio Cortázar do not promote liberation because they subconsciously reflect the mentality of "colonialism." Just as questionable, in Revueltas's mind, are writers such as Gabriel García Márquez and Juan Rulfo, who promote a literature based on the "unreal" and one that is condemned to repetitive modeling. In short, Latin American literature, which is totally alienated from universal culture, must dissolve its alienated state in the same way that Latin America must seek liberation from foreign imperialism, while integrating itself into the international scene.

Politics

Revueltas's political essays are the least studied of his literary works. This neglect is due in large part to the unfortunate fact that many of these important and interesting documents have yet to be published. The political concerns treated in these essays are many: the international Communist movement, the struggle of Third World nations, nuclear war, and the future of socialism, to name but a few. Perhaps the single most important topic, however, that preoccupied Revueltas for some twenty-five years was the status of the Mexican Communist party within Mexican politics. His constant analysis of the directions and policies of the Party that he both loved and hated provided the central focus of his political essays, as well as his fiction, from roughly 1941 to 1965.

Although Revueltas's essays are often obscure and difficult to comprehend by those not possessing an intimate knowledge of such matters, there is a coherent trajectory of original thought running throughout his political essays that was, in large measure, before its time in Latin America. The passion with which Revueltas immersed himself in political thought is ever-present in these works. Revueltas's critical rebelliousness in the face of Mexican political realities has led Enrique González Rojo to observe that Revueltas's profession was "that of being the organizer of a crusade against the disguises with which both the bourgeoisie and all the national political forces hide their identity."[25]

One of Revueltas's earliest political essays, "The National Reality in the Light of Historical Materialism," was published in 1938.[26] Its primary purpose was to analyze the Mexican Revolution from a Marxist perspective. There is a careful tracing of the development and evolution of Mexico's class structure from the colonial period to the Revolution, along with the attendant class struggles. Revueltas argued that the Mexican Revolution signaled the emergence of the proletariat as an organized and potent historical force. He observed that Marxism must provide Mexico's working classes with a theoretical orientation. Interestingly enough, Revueltas also observed that Marxism, in order to succeed as an enlightened movement, must always remain nondogmatic and cognizant of national idiosyncrasies. Thus revisionism, which was to be an organizing principle for his literature and his political activities, was hinted at even in his earliest essays.

Many examples of Revueltas's early political essays, like his essays on aesthetics, appeared as newspaper articles in El Popular from 1941-42. During these years he was concerned with the international crisis in Europe.[27] In 1943, with his expulsion from the Party and the cessation of his work with El Popular, Revueltas turned his attention to the production of political commentaries in two different opposition journals: El Partido (1943-44) and El Insurgente (1944). After these shortlived attempts to promote change in the Party from outside its ranks, Revueltas greatly reduced his activity in the political essay for several years.

In conjunction with his participation in the preliminary work for the creation of the Popular party, Revueltas wrote, in 1947, "The Necessity of New Political Parties in Mexico."[28] This article, as yet unpublished, argues that Mexico lacked a legitimate party to reflect the needs and concerns of the proletariat. He entirely dismissed the idea of the Mexican Communist party as a representative force of socialism. Two years later, after the creation of the Popular party, Revueltas returned to his concern for the formation of a party true to Marxism, but this time he directed his observations directly to Vicente Lombardo Toledano, the leader of the Popular party. The result was "Memorandum Concerning 'The Situation of the Country and the Tasks of the Marxist Movement in Mexico.'"29 In this work Revueltas revealed that his revisionist clamorings were directed not only to the Mexican Communist party, but also to the newly formed Popular party.

In 1950 Revueltas published one of his best political essays, "The Possibilities and Limitations of the Mexican."30 This was an attempt to interpret Mexico's history and its people by means of an elaborate framework based on the principles of historical materialism. Tracing the development of class conflict and economic interest in Mexico, Revueltas methodically dissected his nation's internal contradictions, peculiarities, and inequities. From the standpoint of style, clarity, and persuasiveness, this essay ranks as one of Revueltas's most impressive.

After Revueltas's public denunciation of his literary works in 1950, he all but ceased writing political essays until his reentrance into the Party in 1956. Soon thereafter, Revueltas began a vigorous and intensive internal struggle with the Party's leadership. The result was a torrent of essays that were limited in circulation to mimeographed versions and inexpensive pamphlets.31 These works are of immense importance in clarifying Revueltas's political development between 1956 and 1960, which, in turn, led to his final

expulsion from the Communist party. As a result
of the so-called "secret speech" of Khrushchev in
1957, Revueltas took advantage of the new
freedoms that were apparently emerging within the
Communist movement. He initiated numerous
critiques of the Mexican Communist party that
were designed to convince his colleagues of their
errors and ineptitude. He suggested, among other
things, that the Party served no useful function as
an instrument of the proletariat. In his view, the
Party had separated itself from the masses and
existed only as an insular unit dedicated to its own
survival. He called for a radical restructuring of
the Party and its policies. Although there is much
repetition in these documents, each one possesses a
unique dimension.

Two of these essays in particular stand out as
influential works. The first, The Historical
Dilemma of the Mexican Communist Party, written
in December 1957 and January 1958, was intended
as a formal presentation to the Party.32 Revueltas
insisted that the Party had reached a critical point
in history in which it had to decide between
radical transformation into an authentic
Marxist-Leninist party or suffer its virtual
liquidation as a political and historical reality in
Mexico. He accused the Party of having developed
abnormally, of rejecting sound theory, and of
failing to shape a collective consciousness for the
working class. He further argued that the Party
should readmit without conditions those members of
the Mexican Workers-Farmers party who had been
previously expelled from the Mexican Communist
party. In the following year he intensified his
attack by writing "Lessons from Defeat," in which
he analyzed the failure of the Communist party to
provide effective leadership in the Railway Workers'

strike in 1958.[33] This essay was particularly important because it afforded Revueltas an opportunity to critique the Party's activities within a practical framework. It was thus more difficult to dismiss those observations than those of his more abstract arguments.

During this same period, Revueltas wrote and published a major political study titled Mexico: A Barbarous Democracy.[34] Unlike the other anti-Party essays already mentioned, this work was an analysis of Mexico's political system with particular reference to the curious practice of tapadismo, whereby the President of Mexico names his successor from the ranks of the Partido Revolucionario Institucional (PRI), thus assuring a continuity of power, while affirming the principle of no-reelection. In the same study, Revueltas considered the role of opposition parties in Mexico, particularly that of the Popular party under the leadership of Vicente Lombardo Toledano. He concluded that all parties in Mexico, with the exception of the PRI, served no useful purpose. He went so far as to accuse the opposition parties of willfully conspiring, in some instances, to disguise motives and attitudes within the political arena.

Soon after his expulsion from the Mexican Communist party in 1960, Revueltas began to write his political masterpiece, A Headless Proletariat, which was published in 1962 with the help of the Liga Leninista Espartaco.[35] This work is Revueltas's best political essay in terms of organization, documentation, clarity, and style. Although it is, at times, both abstract and sophisticated, it is thoroughly readable. Whereas the essays written between 1957 and 1960 tended to concentrate solely on the internal struggles of the Mexican Communist party, A Headless Proletariat is much more panoramic in nature. It is essentially an extensive examination of the history and evolution of Mexico's proletariat.

Revueltas's study begins with the premise that Mexico's proletariat was and is alienated from its natural organized consciousness. To prove his point, he traced the historical emergence of the agrarian and urban working classes in Mexico, beginning with Mexican independence in 1821, through the era of reform in the mid-1850s and 1860s, and continuing on through the Mexican Revolution. For Revueltas, all of these crucial historical periods, and especially the Mexican Revolution, occurred without an organized ideology. Only after the Revolution did such an ideology appear, based on democratic-bourgeois concepts and interest. This new ideology cleverly subsumed the aspirations of the proletariat and, through mystification, promoted itself as a revolutionary ideology and the vanguard of the proletariat. This process was made possible after the Mexican State was crystallized as an organic extension of the PRI. But for Revueltas, the Mexican government was in no way an authentic reflection of the proletariat; rather, it was only a disguised national bourgeoisie consciousness.

Having revealed the fraudulence of the state as a vehicle for an organized proletarian consciousness, Revueltas then examined the Mexican Communist party as an alternative for such leadership. In this case Revueltas found nothing but an historical deformation, leading him to posit the idea of the "historical nonexistence" of the Party. Thus, after dismissing Lombardo's Popular party as opportunistic, Revueltas's conclusion was obvious: Mexico's proletariat was utterly without leadership.

A Headless Proletariat was Revueltas's last major political essay. Between 1962 and 1968 he wrote sparingly on the topic. Then, upon finding himself deeply involved in the Student Movement, he suddenly began a flurry of essays that lasted until 1971. These works, most of which were previously unpublished, have recently been collected and edited under the title Mexico 68: Youth and Revolution.[36] This collection is conveniently divided into three basic categories: (1) those essays dealing specifically with the Student Movement of 1968, its strikes, strategies, and dilemmas; (2) those works concerned with the university and academic self-gestation, an idea that Revueltas borrowed from André Gorz; and (3) those writings produced during Revueltas's imprisonment in Lecumberri.

Most of these works are intensely political and reflect great enthusiasm and passion. Nevertheless, since they primarily deal with issues that are esoteric for most readers, these essays are of limited interest. Furthermore, they shed little light on Revueltas's other literature. In any event, it is clear that during the last part of his literary career Revueltas's political interests had taken new directions.

Chapter Six

Conclusion

This study has insisted upon the intimate relationship between Revueltas's personal life and his literature. Indeed, it is at times difficult to come to terms with many of his works without an accompanying knowledge of Revueltas's biography. His penchant for radical politics, his association with the Mexican Communist party, his unswerving idealism, and his immense intelligence emerge repeatedly in his literary works. Simply stated, Revueltas's extraordinary literature is the product of an extraordinary man whose nearly mythic stature continues to haunt Mexico. Perhaps Revueltas, the man, was best described by José Agustín, while commenting on the role of the artist in Mexico's history. Agustín stated:

> By that time another writer had appeared who not only reflected better, in a more profound way, this transition from the Middle Ages to Modern Cannibalism, but who went to the past, to the future, and who left Mexico such a rich legacy that even yet we are unable to cope with it. I am referring to José Revueltas, who is a unique case in Mexican history. He was a writer, a political man, a gifted philosopher and a prophet. He was a Communist, but a rather unusual one, a Christian-Communist

185

> blend; a perfect, living portrait of
> Dostoyevsky's Prince Mishkin, the
> Idiot.[1]

Revueltas is probably best remembered as a novelist, although his novels are of uneven quality. The trajectory of these works can be conveniently divided into five stages of development that directly reflect the author's political maturation. Walls of Water and The Stone Knife belong to Revueltas's early literary career and are products of an essentially orthodox Marxist. Earthly Days is an expression of unorthodox, anti-Stalinist sentiment. In Some Valley of Tears and The Motives of Cain represent an interim period of orthodoxy. Errors, on the other hand, signals a return to a radical revisionism and an attack upon Party politics. Last, Isolation Cell, written late in Revueltas's career, may best be viewed as an artistic novel that radically departs from its predecessors. In spite of the great unevenness encountered in Revueltas's novelistic production, it is clear that he was an innovator in many ways. While thoroughly politicizing the novel, he contributed much to the new narrative of Mexico.

From a strictly literary standpoint, Revueltas's best work was in the short story. He is often acclaimed as one of Latin America's finest short story writers. His short fiction may be divided into essentially three categories: (1) artistic stories of the late 1930s and the 1940s; (2) stories belonging to a more traditional narrative mode that were written during the 1950s and the 1960s; and (3) those stories produced during the last part of his life which may be described as abstract and philosophical. With few exceptions, Revueltas's stories are devoid of surface politics. Thus, unlike his novels, which often employed politics as a central theme, Revueltas's short stories sought deeper and more universal concerns. Interestingly enough, Revueltas produced numerous such stories that are today uniformly cited as classics of contemporary Mexican fiction.

Considerable attention in this work has been devoted to Revueltas's theater. In part this is because there exists no study whatsoever on the topic. Thus, the information contained in Chapter 4 is presented for the first time to a reading audience. The theater under consideration, while unique and somewhat intriguing, is nevertheless of mediocre quality. Only <u>Quadrant of Solitude</u> and <u>They'll Be Waiting For Us In Abril</u> can be described as works of substance. The other works are interesting more in the way in which they relate to the author's personal life than as substantive works of art.

All aspects of Revueltas's life as an artist and as a political activist can be viewed in his essays. Until now, no attempt has ever been made to order and discuss this large corpus of nonfiction. In fact, the majority of such works are known only to a few specialists. By virtue of an overview, it is possible to say that Revueltas's literary career went far beyond that of his fiction and theater. Throughout his life he never stopped writing on political and aesthetic theory. These works, it is assumed, will receive in the future the critical attention that they so richly deserve.

In conclusion, it is hoped that this study has provided the reader with an introduction to Revueltas's literature, particularly with regard to its expansiveness and its penetrating world-view. It is furthermore wished that the various explanations and analyses contained herein have added to an appreciation of this most important writer. Few men in Latin American letters have, on the one hand, contributed so much but, on the other hand, suffered so much neglect. One thing is certain:

with or without this modest introduction, Revueltas
will continue to gain importance as one of the
central figures in contemporary Mexican literature.

Notes and References

Chapter One

1. Revueltas published these memoirs in two segments in El Rehilete. The first appeared with the subtitle "Memorias" in nos. 14-15 (July-October 1965), pp. 21-24. The second was subtitled "La merced, La Colonia Roma, El Colegio Alemán," no. 20 (June 1967), pp. 39-54. Special note must be made of "Las evocaciones requeridas," Diorama de la cultura (Supplement of Excelsior), 18 April 1976, pp. 8-9. Although the title suggests otherwise, these latter fragments are not from the original articles, but from Revueltas's personal notes made during 1956-57.

2. Two good sources of biographical material are Rosaura Revueltas, Los Revueltas (México, 1980); and José Revueltas, Cartas a María Teresa, ed. María Teresa Retes (Mexico, 1979).

3. Mary Lou Dabdoub, "La maldición de José Revueltas," Revista de las revistas (Supplement of Excelsior), 8 August 1973, p. 5.

4. For reference to Revueltas's participation in this strike, see Valentín Campa, Mi testimonio: experiencias de un comunista mexicano (México: Ediciones de Cultura Popular, 1978), p. 329.

5. In addition to Olivia Peralta, whom he divorced in the early 1940s, he married María Teresa Retes in 1947 and was divorced from her in 1970. He was married to Ema Barrón from 1973 until his death in 1976.

6. Revueltas had six children: Andrea, Fermín, Pablo, and Olivia by Olivia Peralta; Román by María Retes; and Moura by Omega Agüero.

7. For a bibliographic account of Revueltas's early short stories, see Marilyn R. Frankenthaler, "Bibliografía de y sobre José Revueltas," Chasqui 7 (February 1978):49-50.

8. Although shortlived (December 1938 to February 1941), the literary journal Taller was of immense importance in Mexican literary circles. Some of the writers associated with the journal were Octavio Paz, Rafael Solana, Efraín Huerta, José Alvarado, and Juan Gil-Albert. The Taller group afforded Revueltas many and varied contacts with Mexico's leading writers of the day.

9. Although the novel was never recovered, Revueltas published what presumably was the first chapter of the manuscript in Taller, no. 2 (April 1939), pp. 15-27, with the same title, "El quebranto." It was subsequently included in his collection of stories titled God on Earth.

10. El Popular was established in 1938 by Vicente Lombardo Toledano, head of the Confederation of Mexican Workers, with the aid of government subsidies. It ceased publication on 30 November 1961. Although the newspaper was never the official organ of any leftist party, it remained the major Communist forum in Mexico for some twenty-three years. Revueltas's association with El Popular did a great deal to strengthen his reputation as a leftist intellectual.

11. For a full listing of dates and topics, see Frankenthaler, "Bibliografía," pp. 53-58.

12. The Stone Knife was the title given to the English translation of El luto humano by its translator, H.R. Hays. Although Hays's title in no way attempts to be faithful to the original Spanish title, it will be used in the subsequent discussions.

13. El Partido was edited by members of the

José Carlos Mariátegui Cell and was intended as an internal opposition organ within the Mexican Communist party. It was one of the major reasons for Revueltas's expulsion. The dates generally given for the publication's run are November 1943 to February 1944.

14. Financial exigencies dictated Revueltas's scriptwriting. While he deplored the crass commercialism of the film industry, he simultaneously maintained a high regard for film as an art form. The bulk of Revueltas's scriptwriting took place in the 1940s and 1950s, although he worked for the National Cinematographic Bank in the early 1960s and again in the early 1970s. For specific titles and dates, see Edmundo García Riera, Historia documental del cine mexicano (México: Ediciones Era, 1972).

15. Revueltas had an immense admiration for theater, but he considered his efforts in the genre to be failures. Two of his plays, Nos esperan en Abril and Los muertos vivirán, have yet to be performed. Another, Pito Pérez en la hoguera, written in the 1950s, was not performed until shortly before Revueltas's death.

16. Revueltas engaged in polemics with Lombardo Toledano for some three decades. The latter's prestige as a leftist leader was widespread. Revueltas, however, seldom agreed with Lombardo Toledano's political orientation, considering him to have sold out, by and large, to the established political regime.

17. The issue of Socialist Realism is fundamental to Revueltas's literary production. It is discussed at some length in Chapters 2 and 5. Briefly, it should be noted that Socialist Realism is a highly prescriptive form of literary dogma that admits only certain literary devices, content, and point of view. Among other things, it stands (particularly in the 1940s and 1950s) in direct

opposition to the more popular "existential" current so prevalent during the period. In short, any Marxist writer suspected of plying his craft with an existential point of view was resolutely attacked by Party theoreticians.

18. This is one of the most interesting literary documents in Mexican literature. The letter first appeared in the Mexico City newspaper, El Nacional, 16 June 1950 (2d section), pp. 1, 3.

19. The actual date of Nos esperan en Abril is uncertain. One copy of the unpublished manuscript given to me by Revueltas has two different dates, 1956 and 1958. According to Revueltas's recollection, he completed the play in 1956.

20. Obra literaria contains only the novels and short stories written before 1967. It excludes Revueltas's theater and essays.

21. The actual number of dead has been disputed; some sources estimate that as many as three hundred died at Tlatelolco. At any rate, the massacre continues to be one of the most important political events to occur in Mexico during the last four decades.

22. Among the crimes that Revueltas was charged with were sedition, larceny, homicide, assault and battery, inciting rebellion, damage to personal property, and illegally possessing firearms. This wide-ranging list of offenses supposedly represented the various crimes committed by demonstrators in the Student Movement. Revueltas was clearly being identified as the leader of the movement and, as such was responsible for its actions.

23. For an account of the assault upon the students and professors, see Revueltas's letter to Arthur Miller, reprinted in México 68: juventud y revolución (México, 1978), pp. 223-44.

Chapter Two

1. José Alvarado, "La obra de José Revueltas," El Libro y el Pueblo, no. 36 (January 1968), p. 17.

2. Luis Leal, "La nueva narrativa mexicana," Nueva Narrativa Hispanoamericana 2 (January 1972):89.

3. Eduardo Lizalde, "La visión que humaniza la miseria," Diorama de la Cultura (Supplement of Excelsior), 18 April 1976, p. 2.

4. For a sound treatment of Socialist Realism, see Marc Slonim, Soviet Russian Literature: Writers and Problems, 1917-1977, 2d rev. ed. (New York: Oxford University Press, 1977).

5. For an excellent study on Revueltas and existentialism, see Marilyn Frankenthaler, José Revueltas: El solitario solidario (Miami, 1979).

6. Andrea Revueltas, "Plática con Artur London sobre mi padre," Revista de Bellas Artes, no. 29 (September-October 1976), p. 42.

7. Timothy Murad, "Before the Storm: José Revueltas and Beginnings of the New Narrative in Mexico," Modern Language Studies 8 (Winter 1977-78):60.

8. Norma Castro Quiteño, "Oponer al ahora y aquí de la vida, el ahora y aquí de la muerte," in Conversaciones con José Revueltas, ed. Jorge Ruffinelli (Xalapa, México, 1977), p. 87.

9. Adolfo Ortega, "El realismo y el progreso de la literatura mexicana," in Conversaciones con José Revueltas, p. 46.

10. James Irby, "La influencia de William Faulkner en cuatro narradores hispanoamericanos," Master's Thesis, Universidad Nacional Autónoma de México, 1956.

11. Emmanuel Carballo, "Diario público de Emmanuel Carballo: Revueltas uno de los grandes," Diorama de la Cultura (Supplement of Excelsior), 5 November 1967, p. 6.

12. Luis Mario Schneider, "Revive la polémica sobre José Revueltas," in Conversaciones con José Revueltas, pp. 96-97.

13. Castro Quiteño, "Oponer," p. 87.

14. José Agustín, "Epílogo de José Agustín," in José Revueltas, Obra literaria (México, 1967), 2; 638.

15. José Luis Martínez, "Premio Nacional de Literatura 'El luto humano' de José Revueltas," reprinted in Literatura mexicana siglo XX 1910-1949. Primera parte (México: Antigua Libería Robredo, 1949), pp. 221-26.

16. "A propósito de Los muros de agua," Los muros de agua, Obras completas (México, 1978), 1:20.

17. Ibid.

18. Arturo Echeverría L., "Espuma entre Los muros de agua," Letras de México 3, no. 6 (15 June 1941):10.

19. Carballo, "Veinte años después: Los muros de agua," México en la Cultura (Supplement of Novedades), 21 May 1961, p. 2.

20. Echeverría L., "Espuma," p. 10.

21. Los muros de agua, p. 175.

22. H.R. Hays, tr., The Stone Knife (New York, 1947).

23. Leal, "Aspects of the Mexican Novel: From Lizardi to Elizondo," Arizona Quarterly 24, no. 1 (Spring 1968):58.

24. Murad, "Before the Storm," p. 62.

25. Samuel Joseph O'Neill, "Psychological-Literary Techniques in Representative Contemporary Novels of Mexico," Ph.D. diss., University of Maryland, 1965, p. 27.

26. Ibid., p. 94

27. For an excellent treatment of myth and mythic structure in The Stone Knife, see Helia María Sheldon, "'Mythopoesis' en la novelística de

José Revueltas," Ph.D. diss., University of California-Irvine 1976.

28. El luto humano, in Obra literaria, 1:327.

29. For a discussion of the autobiographical elements in Earthly Days, see Ortega, "El realismo y el progreso," pp. 50-51.

30. Los días terrenales, in Obras completas, 3:114.

31. Ibid, p. 175.

32. Jaime Labastida, "José Revueltas: literatura, realidad y política," Revista de Bellas Artes, no. 9 (May-June 1973), p. 39.

33. Los días terrenales, p. 34.

34. Ibid., p. 9.

35. Antonio Prieto, "Una disonancia de José Revueltas," Revista Mexicana de Cultura (Supplement of El Nacional), 27 November 1949, p. 4.

36. Enrique Ramírez y Ramírez, "Sobre una literatura de extravío," El Popular 26 April 1950, p. 4.

37. Raul González García, "José Revueltas--Los días terrenales," Revista Mexicana de Cultura (Supplement of El Nacional), 28 May 1950, p. 11.

38. Ramírez, "Sobre una literatura de extravío," Revista Mexicana de Cultura (Supplement of El Nacional), part 1, 11 June 1950, p. 4; part 2, 18 June 1950, pp. 6, 10, 12; part 3, 25 June 1950, pp. 4, 12.

39. Ibid., part 1, p. 4.

40. Ibid.

41. Ibid., Part 2, p. 6.

42. Miguel Angel Mendoza, "Dos escritores mexicanos frente al existencialismo," México en la Cultura (Supplement of Novedades), 31 July 1949, p. 2.

43. E. Díaz Ruanova, "No he conocido ángeles," in Conversaciones con José Revueltas, pp. 111-14.

44. Mauricio de la Selva, "José Revueltas," in
Diálogos con América (México: Cuadernos
Americanos, 1964), p. 117. This interview was
conducted in 1956.

45. Schneider, "Revive," p. 94.

46. En algún valle de lágrimas, in Obras
completas, 4:106. December 1954 is the date that
Revueltas assigned to the "original" last chapter,
which, however, was not published until the 1979
edition.

47. Carlos E. Turón, "La iconoclastia de José
Revueltas," Cuadernos Americanos 169 (March-April
1970):119.

48. En algún valle de lágrimas, p. 100.

49. Jorge Ruffinelli, José Revueltas (Xalapa,
México, 1977), p. 95.

50. For a good treatment of the "thaw" in
Soviet literature during the post-Stalinist period,
see Slonim, Soviet Russian Literature, pp. 320-37.

51. Realism in Art was written in September
1956 and published in the following year. "Letter
from Budapest" was written during Revueltas's trip
to Budapest in the spring of 1957.

52. Floyd F. Merrell, "Man and His Prisons:
Evolving Patterns in José Revueltas' Narrative,"
Revista de Estudios Hispánicos 11 (May 1977):242.

53. Salvador Reyes Nevares, rev. of Los motivos
de Caín, México en la Cultura (Supplement of
Novedades), 10 November 1957, p. 2.

54. Los motivos de Caín, Obras completas,
5:112.

55. Turón, "La iconoclastia," p. 119.

56. Ibid., p. 121.

57. For a study of the Cain myth in The
Motives of Cain, see Sheldon "Mythopoesis," pp.
195-98.

58. Ruffinelli, José Revueltas, p. 92.

59. For an analysis of the development of Existential Marxism in the 1940s and 1950s, see Mark Poster, Existential Marxism in Postwar France: From Sartre to Althusser (Princeton: Princeton University Press, 1975).

60. Agustín, "Epílogo," p. 643.

61. Merrell, "Man and His Prisons," p. 242.

62. Mateo A. Sáenz, "Revueltas y sus Motivos de Caín," Vida Universitaria, no. 380 (2 July 1958), p. 9.

63. Evodio Escalante, José Revueltas: una literatura del "lado moridor" (México, 1979), p. 14.

64. Los errores, Obra literaria, 2:161-62.

65. Marco Antonio Millán, "Horror y hermosura en Los errores de José Revueltas," El Libro y el Pueblo, no. 3 (April 1965), p. 15. Officially called the Camisas Doradas ("Gold Shirts"), this organization was formed and led by the veteran revolutionary general, Nicolás Rodríguez. Conceived as an ultra right-wing, anti-Semitic, and anti-Communist group, the Gold Shirts had many street skirmishes with Communist groups until it was officially dissolved by orders of President Cárdenas in August 1936. For further information see Campa Mi testimonio, pp. 106-9.

66. "El autoanálisis literario," Cuestionamientos e intenciones, Obras completas, 17:223.

67. García Flores, "La libertad como conocimiento y transformación," in Conversaciones con José Revueltas, p. 74.

68. Los errores, p. 365.

69. Alonso Maldonado, Adriana Salinas, and Teresa Waisman, "Revueltas: Los héroes del error, Crítica Militante 1, no. 1 (March-April 1978):5.

70. For a treatment of the positive hero in Revueltas's novels, see Sam Slick, "The Positive Hero in the Novels of José Revueltas," Ph.D. diss.,

University of Iowa, 1974.
71. Turón, "La iconoclastia," p. 122.
72. Clara Passafari, "José Revueltas y la literatura de protesta social," Boletín de Literaturas Hispánicas (Argentina) no. 7 (1967), p. 18.
73. Ortega, "El realismo," p. 51.
74. Emmanuel Carballo, "La novela y el cuento," La Cultura en México (Suppplement of Siempre), 6 January 1965, p. 3.
75. Mauricio de la Selva, rev. of Los errores, Cuadernos Americanos 136, no. 5 (September–October 1964):278.
76. Carmen Andrade, rev. of Los errores, El Rehilete, no. 13 (April 1965), p. 61.
77. Rev. of Los errores, México en la Cultura (Supplement of Novedades), 23 August 1964, p. 7.
78. Sadot Fabila H., "Los errores, obra para discutir profunda y apasionadamente," El Día, 12 December 1964, p. 11.
79. Dubbed the Palacio Negro, Lecumberri had a reputation as one of Mexico's worst penal institutions, housing many of Mexico's most dangerous criminals, as well as sizable numbers of political prisoners. It was finally closed down in the 1970s.
80. Centro de Investigaciones Linguístico-Literarias, "El apando: Metáfora de la opresión," Texto Crítico, no. 2 (July–December 1975), p. 66.
81. When asked to comment on the people and events in El apando, the author revealed the large extent to which the work is based on fact. The character of El Carajo, for instance, was patterned after a real prisoner named "loco Avitia." For further information, see work cited in previous note, pp. 62–63.
82. Ibid.

83. Manuel Blanco, rev. of El apando, El Nacional, 3 May 1970, p. 6.

84. Argelio Gasca, "José Revueltas: el ojo de la cerradura," Diorama de la Cultura (Supplement of Excelsior), 21 February 1970, p. 12.

85. Juan Tovar, "Lenguaje de nadie, palabra de todos," Diorama de la Cultura (Supplement of Excelsior), 18 April 1976, p. 5.

Chapter Three

1. Luis Leal, "The New Mexican Short Story," Studies in Short Fiction 8 (Winter 1971):12.

2. José Agustín, "Contemporary Mexican Fiction," in Literature and Censorship in Latin America Today: Dream Within a Dream, ed. John Kirk and Don Schmidt (Denver: University of Denver, 1978), p. 18.

3. Fernando Díez de Urdanivia, "La palabra rescatada," El Gallo Ilustrado (Supplement of El Dia), 25 April 1976, p. 2.

4. María Tejera, "Literatura y dialéctica," in Conversaciones con José Revueltas, p. 77.

5. María del Carmen Millán, "José Revueltas," in Antología de cuentos mexicanos (México: Editorial Nueva Imagen, 1977), p. 146.

6. Leal, "Introducción," in Breve historia del cuento mexicano (México: Ediciones de Andrea, 1956), p. 6.

7. For a discussion of this point, see Escalante, José Revueltas, pp. 15–18.

8. Las cenizas was compiled and edited by Andrea Revueltas and Philippe Chéron for inclusion in the Obras completas. It includes previously unpublished short stories, those that were published posthumously, Revueltas's poetry, as well as his previously published fragments of novels.

9. Antonio Sánchez Barbudo, rev. of <u>Dios en la</u> <u>tierra, El Hijo Pródigo</u> 6, no. 20 (15 November 1944):121.

10. Alí Chumacero, "José Revueltas," <u>Letras de</u> <u>México</u> 4, no. 24 (10 December 1944):5.

11. "La caída" and "Verde es el color de la esperanza" were first published in <u>Dios en la tierra.</u> For a bibliography of the other fourteen stories, see "Apéndice bibliográfico," in <u>Dios en la tierra,</u> <u>Obras completas,</u> 8:171-76.

12. Murad, "Before the Storm," p. 63.

13. Leal, <u>Breve historia,</u> p. 139.

14. Labastida, "José Revueltas," p. 36.

15. Agustín, "Epílogo," p. 646.

16. In an interview with Ignacio Solares in 1974, Revueltas cited "The Incredible Frontier" as his favorite short story. He also discussed the story's inspiration, a book by Chekhov on Dostoyevsky, which apparently gave Revueltas a new perspective on the age-old question of life versus death. See Ignacio Solares, "La verdad es siempre revolucionaria," in <u>Conversaciones con José</u> <u>Revueltas,</u> p. 59.

17. Revueltas published three different stories titled "La frontera increíble." The first, already discussed, appeared initially in <u>Revista de</u> <u>Guatamala</u> 3 (January-March 1946):47-52. The second was published in <u>Letras de México</u> 6, no. 131 (February 1947):33-36. It was later renamed "Lo que sólo uno escucha," for inclusion in <u>Dormir</u> <u>en tierra.</u> Yet a third story appeared under the same title in <u>Orígenes</u> (Havana), no. 14 (Summer 1947), pp. 25-27.

18. Timothy Murad, "José Revueltas in the Mexican Short Story," Ph.D. diss., Rutgers University, 1975, p. 234.

19. Díez, "La palabra," p. 2.

20. Revueltas used a version of this plot in Quadrant of Solitude, but in the play it is a student who implicates himself to save his teacher from dismissal (see Chapter 4).

21. For an excellent study of time and space in "The Sacred Word," see Edith Negrín, "'La palabra sagrada' de Revueltas: tiempo, espacio y sociedad," Texto Crítico, no. 11 (September–December 1978), pp. 165–80.

22. For an incisive study of the thematic role of language in "The Language of the Dispossessed," see Márgara Russotto, "Realismo, lenguaje y significado: reflexiones sobre un cuento de Revueltas," Cuadernos Americanos 210 (January–February 1977):233–46.

23. Labastida, "José Revueltas," p. 37.

24. José de la Colina, "Un oscuro canto relampagueante," Plural, 15 June 1974, p. 77.

25. Ibid.

26. Ruffinelli, José Revueltas, p. 123.

27. Luis Arturo Ramos, "El tiempo y la anécdota en Material de los sueños," La Palabra y el Hombre 13 (January–March 1975):72.

28. "The Massacre of the Madmen," tr. W.H. Clamurro, Review, nos. 21-22 (Fall-Winter 1977), pp. 158–59.

29. For a good study of the role of language in "Bed No. 11," see Luis Arturo Ramos, "Revueltas y el grotesco," Texto Crítico, no. 2 (July-December 1975), pp. 67–80.

30. Material de los sueños, Obras completas, 10:41.

31. The following explanatory note was written by Revueltas on the original manuscript. Given its delicate philosophical message, it has been left in the original: "Teoría del también de los otros y de las cosas, el también otro del yo, la otredad del

también y del otro de la cosa y de la cosa y el yo." See "Apéndice Bibliográfico," Material de los sueños, n.p.

32. Revueltas had planned to write a novel entitled Hegel and I, but, upon his death, no trace of such a project surfaced in his private papers. In all probability, only the short story, "Hegel y yo," was ever realized for the projected novel.

33. "Apéndice Bibliográfico," Material de los sueños, n.p.

34. Ibid.

35. Ortega, "El realismo," p. 48.

36. Escalante, José Revueltas, p. 109.

37. Ramos, "El tiempo y la anécdota," p. 71.

Chapter Four

1. At this writing, Ediciones Era of Mexico City has contracted to publish all five plays by Revueltas.

2. "Teatro, hombre y sociedad," Diorama de la Cultura (Supplement of Excelsior), 26 August 1973, p. 2.

3. For background information and lists of performances concerning La Linterna Mágica, as well as Revueltas's involvement with the group, see Antonio Magaña Esquivel, Sueño y realidad del teatro (México: Instituto Nacional de Bellas Artes, 1949), pp. 85-92.

4. Israel (México, n.d.).

5. Salvador Novo, La vida en México en el período presidencial de Miguel Alemán (México: Empresas Editoriales, S.A., 1967), p. 181.

6. Fletcher's first name, Jhonaton, is typical of many renderings of English names and words which occur in the published text: Wrigth for Wright, wont for want, and so forth.

7. John B. Nomland, Teatro mexicano contemporáneo (México: Instituto Nacional de Bellas Artes, 1967), p. 294.

8. In a personal interview on 5 August 1975 Revueltas reflected, with considerable humor, upon the amateurish qualities of Israel. He was particularly amused with Act III and his use of an oil pipeline as the setting, admitting freely his own naiveté concerning the size of such conduits.

9. Manuel Lerín, "Un drama de José Revueltas," El Nacional, 2 January 1948, p.7.

10. Thelma Ortiz, rev. of Israel, Books Abroad 25 (1951):60.

11. Israel, p. 30.

12. Magaña Esquivel, Sueño y realidad del teatro, p. 91.

13. The year of Quadrant's debut has been inaccurately reported as 1953 in various articles.

14. El cuadrante de la soledad (México, 1971).

15. Frank Dauster, rev. of El cuadrante de la soledad, Handbook of Latin American Studies, no. 36 (1974), p. 440.

16. El cuadrante de la soledad, n.p. The announcement was included at the beginning of the published script, under the heading "El autor se propone denunciar."

17. Ibid.

18. Miguel Guardia, rev. of El cuadrante de la soledad, México en la Cultura (Supplement of Novedades), 21 May 1950, p. 4.

19. Magaña Esquivel, rev. of El cuadrante de la soledad, Revista Mexicana de Cultura (Supplement of El Nacional), 21 May 1950, p. 13.

20. Rafael Solana, rev. of El cuadrante de la soledad, Hoy, 27 May 1950, p. 18.

21. Juan Almagre, rev. of El cuadrante de la soledad, El Nacional, 8 June 1950, p. 3.

22. Ibid.

23. "Carta abierta de José Revueltas," El Nacional, 11 June 1950, p. 1.

24. Ibid.

25. Almagre, "Respueta a una respuesta de José Revueltas: No se puede servir a dos amos," El Nacional, 14 June 1950, p. 7.

26. Ibid.

27. The content and impact of Ramírez's three-part series, "Sobre una literatura de extravío," is discussed in Chapter 2.

28. "El escritor José Revueltas hace importante aclaración," El Nacional, 16 June 1950, pp. 1,3.

29. Ibid., p. 3.

30. Personal interview with Revueltas, 5 August 1975.

31. Pito Pérez en la hoguera TS, n.d., p.1.

32. Ibid., p. 39.

33. Malkah Rabell, "Querido, querido Revueltas, hasta pronto," El Gallo Ilustrado (Supplement of El Día), 25 April 1976, p. 4.

34. Ignacio Hernández, "José Revueltas: balance existencial," in Conversaciones con José Revueltas, p. 29.

35. Pito Pérez TS, p. 39.

36. Ibid.

37. Ibid.

38. Agustín, "Epílogo," p. 643.

39. Hernández, "José Revueltas," p. 31.

40. Ibid.

41. Agustín, "Epílogo," p. 643.

42. Nos esperan en Abril TS, p. 22.

43. My thanks to Andrea Revueltas and Philippe Chéron for providing a typescript version of the manuscript.

44. Cartas a María Teresa, pp. 35-39.

45. Personal interview with Revueltas, 5 August

1975.

Chapter Five

1. Ediciones Era plans to publish all of Revueltas's unpublished essays in future volumes of his Obras completas.
2. Rodolfo Rojas Zea, "Despedida en la C.U. a José Revueltas. El escritor y político falleció ayer en el Instituto de la Nutrición," Excelsior, 15 April 1976, p. 19.
3. Andrea Revueltas and Philippe Chéron, "Presentacion," in José Revueltas, Cuestionamientos e intenciones, Obras completas, 18:9.
4. Russotto, "Realismo," p. 235.
5. "Un juicio de Juan Ramón Jiménez: América sombría," El Popular, 13 March 1942, pp. 5-6.
6. "Réplica sobre la novela: El cascabel al gato," El Popular, 23 May 1943, p. 3.
7. "La novela, tarea de México," Letras de México 5, no. 128 (October 1946):337-38, 348-49.
8. "Esquema sobre las cuestiones del materialismo dialéctico y la estética a propósito de Los días terrenales," in Cuestionamientos e intenciones, pp. 32-46.
9. El realismo en el arte (México, 1956).
10. "Carta de Budapest a los escritores comunistas," in Cuestionamientos, pp. 70-81.
11. "A propósito de Los muros de agua" (see note 16, Chapter 2).
12. "Respecto a una conotación revolucionaria del arte," in Cuestionamientos, pp. 82-86.
13. "Un personaje de Gide y algunas ideas sobre el arte," in Cuestionamientos, pp. 192-99.
14. El conocimiento cinematográfico y sus problemas (México, 1965).
15. "El autoanálisis literario" (see note 66,

Chapter 2).

16. "Esquema teórico para un ensayo sobre las cuestiones del arte y la libertad," in Cuestionamientos, pp. 186-91.

17. "Un 'toque de queda' soviético contra la libre expresión del pensamiento," in Cuestionamientos, pp. 200-206.

18. "Prólogo del autor a la presente edición," Obra literaria, 1:7-16.

19. "Mi posición esencial," in Cuestionamientos, pp. 236-40. This essay was originally delivered as a lecture in 1966.

20. "Problemas del conocimiento estético," in Cuestionamientos, pp. 154-72.

21. "Escuela mexicana de pintura y novela de la revolución," in Cuestionamientos, pp. 241-74.

22. This prologue is included in Cuestionamientos e intenciones (pp. 135-53), not as a prologue to the book but as one of the many essays on art.

23. Two works from this period, in particular, deserve mention: "Teatro, hombre y sociedad," Diorama de la Cultura (Supplement of Excelsior), 26 August 1973, pp. 2-5; and "El oficio de escritor," reprinted in Cuestionamientos, pp. 319-25. "Teatro" is a reworked version of a lecture originally delivered in 1953. "El oficio," also a lecture, was delivered in 1975 and published in the same year.

24. "Literatura y liberación en América Latina," in Cuestionamientos, pp. 287-318. This essay, first published in 1975, is a combination of two lectures delivered by Revueltas in 1972, the second of which is a reworked version of a lecture originally delivered in Havana in 1968 and published in 1971.

25. Enrique González Rojo, "Homenaje a José Revueltas: Su obra política," Los Universitarios,

nos. 70-71 (April 1976), p. 4.

26. "La realidad nacional a la luz del materialismo histórico," Acción Social 1, no. 3 (August 1938):4-16.

27. For a complete listing of these articles see Frankenthaler, "Bibliografía," pp. 53-57.

28. "La necesidad de nuevos partidos políticos en México." A typescript of this essay was provided on microfilm by the Revueltas family.

29. "Memorandum sobre 'La situación del país y las tareas del movimiento marxista en México.'" Typescript was provided on microfilm.

30. "Posibilidades y limitaciones del mexicano," Filosofía y Letras 20, no. 40 (October-December 1950):255-73.

31. Many of these works were given to me on microfilm by the Revueltas family. It is assumed that these essays were reproduced in some fashion, probably mimeographed, and circulated among political intimates of Revueltas. Some representative titles are "La crítica está en marcha y ya nadie podrá detenerla" (1957); "El sentido real de una línea política" (1957-58); "Algunos aspectos de la vida del Partido Comunista Mexicano" (1957); "La situación actual del Partido y las tareas relacionadas con su transformación en un verdadero partido marxista-leninista del proletariado" (coauthored with David Alfaro Siqueiros, 1957); "Balance de la lucha interna y las actividades de la misma después de la derrota del movimiento ferrocarrilero" (1959); "Medio paso adelante . . . y un salto mortal hacia atrás" (1959); and "El culto a la espontaneidad en el Partido Comunista Mexicano" (1959).

32. This work is reported in several bibliographies as a written text titled La disyuntiva histórica del Partido Comunista Mexicano and

published by the Central Committee of the PCM in 1958. A search has failed to yield such a document. There is, however, a microfilmed copy of a published version of this presentation under the title El Partido Comunista Mexicano ante la disyuntiva vital de su existencia histórica. The document indicates that it was published by Ediciones Liga Leninista Espartaco in 1965. Revueltas noted in this edition that the original presentation was totally rejected by the PCM. It is highly doubtful, therefore, that it was ever published by the party, as has been reported.

33. "Enseñanzas de una derrota," Revolución, no. 4 (June 1960), pp. 7-20. This work was written in April 1959.

34. México: Una democracia bárbara (México, 1958).

35. Ensayo sobre un proletariado sin cabeza, vol. 17 of Obras completas.

36. México 68: juventud y revolución, vol. 15 of Obras completas.

Chapter Six

1. Agustín, "Contemporary Mexican Fiction," pp. 16-17.

Selected Bibliography

Primary Sources

Given the large number of works involved, an extensive bibliography of Revueltas is precluded by space limitations. Thus, only major works are listed below. In the case of multiple publications, excluding those also available in collected works, only the most recent has been cited. For bibliographic information concerning Revueltas's minor works, the reader is directed to Marilyn Frankenthaler's "Bibliografía de y sobre José Revueltas" (see Secondary Sources). With the exception of the theater works, unpublished items have not been included since they are not currently available.

1. Collected Works

Obras completas. Edited by Andrea Revueltas and Philippe Chéron. México: Ediciones Era, 1978-. This collection is still in the process of being edited. The publisher's contract calls for the entire collection to consist of twenty-five volumes. Whenever possible, this study has utilized the works published in the Obras completas. To date, fourteen volumes are available: 1. Los muros de agua, 1978; 2. El luto humano, 1980; 3. Los días terrenales, 1979; 4. En algún valle de lágrimas, 1979; 5. Los motivos de Caín, 1979; 6. Los errores, 1979; 7. El apando, 1978; 8. Dios en la tierra,1979; 9. Dormir en tierra, 1978; 10. Material

de los sueños, 1979; 11. Las cenizas,1981;
15. México 68: juventud y revolución,1978;
17. Ensayo sobre un proletariado sin cabeza,
1980; and 18. Cuestion amientos e intenciones, 1978.
Obra literaria. 2 vols. México: Empresas
 Editoriales, 1967. This collection includes
 all of the novels and most of the short
 stories written prior to 1967. It does
 not, however, include any essays or
 theater works.

2. Novels and Short Story Collections
El apando. México: Ediciones Era, 1971.
Los días terrenales. México: Ediciones Era, 1973.
Dios en la tierra. México: Editorial Novaro, 1973.
Dormir en tierra. México: Ediciones Era, 1971.
En algún valle de lágrimas. México: Editorial
 Novaro, 1973.
Los errores. México: Fondo de Cultura Económica,
 1964.
El luto humano. México: Editorial Novaro, 1972.
Material de los sueños. México: Ediciones Era,
 1974.
Los motivos de Caín. Buenos Aires: Editorial
 Galerna, 1967.
Los muros de agua. México: Editorial Novaro, 1973.

3. Theater Works
El cuadrante de la soledad. México: Editorial
 Novaro, 1971.
Israel. México: Sociedad General de Autores de
 México, n.d.
Los muertos vivirán. TS., 1947.
Nos esperan en Abril. TS., 1956.
Pito Pérez en la hoguera. TS., n.d.

4. Major Essays

El conocimiento cinematográfico y sus problemas. México: Universidad Nacional Autónoma de México, 1965.

Ensayo sobre un proletariado sin cabeza. México: Ediciones Leninista Espartaco, 1962.

México: Una democracia bárbara. Posibilidades y limitaciones del Mexicano. México: Editorial Posada, 1975.

El Partido Comunista Mexicano ante la disyuntiva vital de su existencia histórica. México: Ediciones Liga Leninista Espartaco, 1965.

El realismo en el arte. México: n.p., 1956.

Secondary Sources

Agustín, José. "Epílogo de José Agustín." Vol. 2 of *Obra literaria.* By José Revueltas. México: Empresas Editoriales, S.A., 1967, pp. 631–48. A good introduction to Revueltas's narrative prior to 1967.

Centro de Investigaciones Lingüístico–Literarias. "*El apando*: Metáfora de la opresión." *Texto Crítico*, no. 2 (July–December 1975), pp. 40–66. A major study of structure and meaning in *El apando*.

Dabdoub, Mary Lou. "La maldición de José Revueltas." *Revista de las Revistas* (Supplement of Excelsior), 8 Aug. 1973, pp. 5–9. A particularly good interview, noteworthy for Revueltas's personal views on many matters.

Escalante, Evodio. *José Revueltas: una literatura del "lado moridor."* México: Ediciones Era, S.A. 1979. An important contribution to Revueltian studies, employing a Deleuzian approach.

Frankenthaler, Marilyn R. "Bibliografía de y sobre
   José Revueltas." Chasqui 7, no. 2 (February
   1978):46-93. This study is an invaluable
   source; it eclipses in scope all previous
   bibliographies on Revueltas.
Frankenthaler, Marilyn R. José Revueltas: El
   Solitario solidario. Miami: Ediciones
   Universal, 1979. A major study on
   existentialism in the works of José
   Revueltas.
González Rojo, Enrique. "Homenaje a José
   Revueltas: su obra política." Los
   Universitarios, nos. 70-71 (April 1976),
   pp. 4-6. The best study available on
   Revueltas's political life.
Hays, H.R., trans. The Stone Knife. By José
   Revueltas. New York: Reynal and Hitchcock,
   1947. A respectable translation of El
   luto humano. This is the only major work
   of Revueltas's fiction ever to be trans-
   lated into English.
Irby, James E. "La influencia de William Faulkner
   en cuatro narradores hispanoamericanos."
   Master's Thesis. Universidad Nacional
   Autónoma de México, 1956. One of
   the first academic studies of Revueltas's
   narrative.
Labastida, Jaime. "José Revueltas: literatura,
   realidad y política." Revista de Bellas
   Artes, no. 9 (May-June 1973), pp. 31-40.
   A good introductory article on Revueltas's
   narrative.
Merrell, Floyd F. "Man and His Prisons: Evolving
   Patterns in José Revueltas' Narrative."
   Revista de Estudios Hispánicos, 11 (May
   1977):233-250. An insightful study of the
   themes of physical and existential
   incarceration in Revueltas's novels.
Murad, Timothy. "Before the Storm: José Revueltas

and Beginnings of the New Narrative in
Mexico." Modern Language Studies 8
(Winter 1977-78):57-64. A seminal study
that elucidates Revueltas's role in
the development of contemporary Mexican
literature.

Murad, Timothy. "José Revueltas in the Mexican
Short Story." Ph.D. diss., Rutgers
University, 1975. A thorough analysis of
Revueltas's short fiction.

Negrín, Edith. "'La palabra sagrada' de Revueltas:
tiempo, espacio y sociedad." Texto Crítico, no.
11 (September–December 1978), pp. 165-80. An
award-winning essay on one of Revueltas's
most important short stories.

O'Neill, Samuel Joseph. "Psychological-Literary
Techniques in Representative Contemporary
Novels of Mexico." Ph.D. diss., University
of Maryland, 1965. Pages 24-141 contain the
best stylistic and structural analysis
available on El luto humano.

Ramírez y Ramírez, Enrique. "Sobre una literatura
de extravío." Revista Mexicana de
Cultura (Supplement of El Nacional),
part I, 11 June 1950, p. 4; part II, 18
June 1950, pp. 6, 10, 12; part III,
25 June 1950, pp. 4, 12. This series
of articles is included here because of
its fundamental importance in understanding the controversies surrounding Los días
terrenales and El cuadrante de la soledad.

Retes, María Teresa, ed. Cartas a María Teresa.
México: Premiã editora, 1979. An impressive
compilation of letters written by Revueltas
to his second wife between 1947 and 1972.

Revueltas, Andrea and Chéron, Phillipe,
"Presentación." Cuestionamientos e
intenciones. Vol. 18 of Obras
completas. By José Revueltas. México: Ediciones

Era, S.A. 1978, pp. 9-20. A highly informative introduction to Revueltas's writings on aesthetics.

Revueltas, Rosaura. Los Revueltas. México: Editorial Grijalbo, S.A., 1980. A somewhat uneven history of the Revueltas family. Pages 133-182 deal with José.

Ruffinelli, Jorge, ed. Conversaciones con José Revueltas. Xalapa, México: Universidad Veracruzana, 1977. An absolutely essential work for those interested in Revueltas. It contains thirteen key interviews given by Revueltas from 1950 to 1976. Also included in this work is Frankenthaler's "Bibliografía," pp. 115-53.

Ruffinelli, Jorge. José Revueltas. Xalapa, México: Universidad Veracruzana, 1977. The first book-length study ever published on Revueltas. Although it is limited just to narrative works, it is a valuable source of information.

Russotto, Márgara. "Realismo, lenguaje y significado: reflexiones sobre un cuento de Revueltas." Cuadernos Americanos 210 (January-February 1977):233-46. A particularly impressive study of Revueltas's "El lenguaje de nadie."

Sheldon, Helia María. "'Mythopoesis' en la novelística de José Revueltas." Ph.D. diss., University of California, Irvine, 1976. An important study of myth and symbolism in El luto humano and Los días terrenales.

Slick, Samuel L. "The Positive Hero in the Novels of José Revueltas." Ph.D. diss., University of Iowa, 1974. This study attempts to trace the evolution of Party heroes in Revueltas's novels, from orthodoxy to rebellion.

Turón, Carlos, E. "La iconoclastia de José Revueltas." Cuadernos Americanos 169, no.

2 (March–April 1970):97–125. An important
study that analyzes Revueltas's <u>persona</u>
in his novels.

Index

a 863.44
R 454

115 807

DATE DUE

GAYLORD			PRINTED IN U.S.A.